(Continued)

Early Childhood Education Series titles, continued

The Play's the Thing:
Teachers' Roles in Children's Play
ELIZABETH JONES & GRETCHEN REYNOLDS

Scenes from Day Care
ELIZABETH BALLIETT PLATT

Raised in East Urban
CAROLINE ZINSSER

Play and the Social Context of Development in Early
Care and Education
BARBARA SCALES, MILLIE ALMY, AGELIKI NICOLOPOULOU,
& SUSAN ERVIN-TRIPP, Eds.

The Whole Language Kindergarten
SHIRLEY RAINES & ROBERT CANADY

Children's Play and Learning
EDGAR KLUGMAN & SARA SMILANSKY

Serious Players in the Primary Classroom
SELMA WASSERMANN

Young Children Continue to Reinvent Arithmetic—
2nd Grade
CONSTANCE KAMII

The Good Preschool Teacher
WILLIAM AYERS

A Child's Play Life: An Ethnographic Study
DIANA KELLY-BYRNE

The War Play Dilemma
NANCY CARLSSON-PAIGE & DIANE E. LEVIN

The Piaget Handbook for Teachers and Parents
ROSEMARY PETERSON &VICTORIA FELTON-COLLINS

Promoting Social and Moral Development in Young
Children
CAROLYN POPE EDWARDS

Today's Kindergarten
BERNARD SPODEK, Ed.

Visions of Childhood
JOHN CLEVERLEY & D. C. PHILLIPS

Starting School
NANCY BALABAN

Ideas Influencing Early Childhood Education
EVELYN WEBER

The Joy of Movement in Early Childhood
SANDRA R. CURTIS

The Power of Projects

MEETING CONTEMPORARY CHALLENGES
IN EARLY CHILDHOOD CLASSROOMS—
STRATEGIES AND SOLUTIONS

Edited by

JUDY HARRIS HELM
SALLEE BENEKE

Teachers College
Columbia University
New York and London

National Association
for the Education of
Young Children

Published simultaneously by Teachers College Press, 1234 Amsterdam Avenue, New York, NY 10027 and the National Association for the Education of Young Children, 1509 16th Street NW, Washington, DC 20036-1426

Library of Congress Cataloging-in-Publication Data

The power of projects : meeting contemporary challenges in early childhood classrooms—strategies and solutions / edited by Judy Harris Helm and Sallee Beneke.
       p.   cm. — (Early childhood education series)
   Includes bibliographical references and index.
   ISBN 0-8077-4298-8 (pbk. : alk. paper)
   1. Project method in teaching.   2. Early childhood education—Curricula.
I. Helm, Judy Harris.   II. Beneke, Sallee.   III. Early childhood education series (Teachers College Press)
   LB1139.35.P8 P69   2002
   372.1102–dc21   2002026793

ISBN 0-8077-4298-8 (paper)
NAEYC order number 211

Printed on acid-free paper
Manufactured in the United States of America

10   09   08   07   06   05   04   03   8 7 6 5 4 3 2 1

Contents

Acknowledgments   vii

1. Contemporary Challenges in Early Childhood Education   1
Judy Harris Helm

2. Building a Good Foundation for Children   10
Lilian G. Katz

3. Overcoming the Ill Effects of Poverty   19

Defining the Challenge,
by *Judy Harris Helm*   19

Practical Strategies,
by *Judy Harris Helm and Jean Lang*   20

The Airplane Project, by *Jean Lang*   25

4. Moving Young Children Toward Literacy   34

Defining the Challenge,
by *Judy Harris Helm*   34

Practical Strategies,
by *Mary Ann Gottlieb*   35

The Water to River Project,
by *Jean O'Mara Thieman*   42

5. Responding to Children's Special Needs   50

Defining the Challenge,
by *Judy Harris Helm and Sallee Beneke*   50

Practical Strategies,
by *Pam Scranton and Sharon Doubet*   51

The Bird Project, by *Pam Scranton*   57

6. Supporting Second-Language Learners   64

Defining the Challenge,
by *Judy Harris Helm and Rebecca A. Wilson*   64

Practical Strategies,
by *Rebecca A. Wilson*   65

The Mexican Restaurant Project,
by *Rebecca A. Wilson*   71

7. Meeting Standards Effectively   79

Defining the Challenge,
by *Judy Harris Helm and Sallee Beneke*   79

Practical Strategies, by *Sallee Beneke*   80

The Pizza Project, by *Marilyn Worsley*   86

8. The Importance of Documentation   97
Judy Harris Helm

9. Future Challenges: Concluding Thoughts   103
Judy Harris Helm

Appendix A: Frequently Asked Questions and Practical Advice   105

Appendix B: Recommended Resources   115

About the Editors and Contributors   117

Index   119

Acknowledgments

The editors and contributors wish to acknowledge the staff and parents of the schools and centers discussed in this book for generously sharing their children's work. These include Bright Beginnings, Woodford County Special Education Association, Eureka, Illinois; Discovery Preschool, Northminster Presbyterian Church, Peoria, Illinois; Illinois Valley Community College Child Care Program, Oglesby, Illinois; Rockford Early Childhood Program, Rockford, Illinois; West Liberty Dual Language Program, West Liberty, Iowa; and Valeska Hinton Early Childhood Education Center, Peoria, Illinois. Dianne Rothenberg and Lilian Katz, at the ERIC Clearinghouse on Elementary and Early Childhood Education, and Char Ward, at Starnet Regions I and III at Western Illinois University, have supported collaborative work and training related to *The Power of Projects*. Several readers reviewed early drafts and provided excellent advice. These included Beatrice Colon, Early Childhood Education Consultant, on bilingual education for the Illinois State Board of Education; Carol Copple, National Association for the Education of Young Children; Lila Goldston, Center for Early Childhood Leadership, National-Louis University, on cultural issues; and Joan Gore Krupa, Director of Heartland Community Health Clinic, on parent/community issues. Additional editorial assistance was provided by Amanda Helm. The editors are extremely grateful for the support and advice of Susan Liddicoat, acquisitions editor at Teachers College Press. This book was complex and produced in a short time by numerous writers. Without her guidance, encouragement, and patience this book would never have happened. And last but not least, the editors wish to acknowledge the support of not only their spouses and children but the families of all the contributors. Participation in a "community of practice" dedicated to doing the right thing for children and families takes time and commitment. We are blessed by family members who believe in and support our community and the work we do.

CHAPTER 1

Contemporary Challenges in Early Childhood Education

Judy Harris Helm

The kindergarten teacher commented on the changes in the terrain as the van drove northward through the mountains of Kentucky. The interest in the changing topography was brief, however, because the discussion inside the van was charged. These were teachers, administrators, and teacher educators returning to Illinois from the annual conference of the National Association for the Education of Young Children (NAEYC) in Atlanta. The participants were excited about new ideas and plans to try different teaching approaches. Books purchased in the exhibit hall were passed around and discussed. Every member of the group had participated in "A Night of Sharing," at which projects completed by children, prekindergarten through second grade, were displayed and discussed. These early childhood professionals reported on concerns teachers had shared and examined their own attitudes toward innovation.

"One teacher was very concerned about what was happening in the state in which she taught. She seemed convinced that standards would mean the end of engaged teaching strategies like projects."

"I had several interesting conversations with teachers about how to cover curriculum goals by doing projects."

"I didn't have any conversations with teachers about standards, but I did have several discussions about children with special needs. Several teachers felt that projects were an inappropriate way to help children with special needs meet Individual Education Plan (IEP) goals. One teacher told me that she couldn't do project work because she had a child with autism in her classroom this year. She about fell over when I told her

that I had two children with autism in my class when we did the Grocery Store Project. We spent a lot of time looking at the autistic children's portfolios, and I pointed to evidence of how effectively their IEP goals had been met through project work. I think she is going to try a project."

"A teacher told me that he was surprised to see the project we did in my bilingual classroom. We had a great conversation; he demonstrated on my documentation panels how some of the activities that we did in our project are actually recommended strategies for children learning English as a second language."

"Did you ever notice how sometimes we as teachers get into the 'yes, buts'? 'Projects are good BUT I have children with special needs.' 'Yes, BUT I have children who are learning a second language.' 'Yes, BUT I have these standards to cover.' 'Yes, BUT I have to teach the children to read in first grade.' I do that all the time when I first learn about a different way of doing things."

"The one I try hardest to avoid is the 'Yes, BUT my children have so many challenges in their lives. I really need to spend all of my time on drill and practice, on the basics, just so they will survive.' It really scares me when I think like that, because it means that I am in danger of keeping from these children the opportunity to do other things, especially more higher-level thinking, like investigative work."

"If children aren't challenged to think, it can become a self-fulfilling prophecy. If children don't get a chance to be curious and find answers to their questions, they don't see themselves as successful learners, or they don't view school as a place where they can learn interesting, relevant things. Eventually, their intellectual curiosity dies."

"Teachers are overwhelmed. We are all overwhelmed with the challenges we face in teaching today. I get scared sometimes thinking about how much the decisions we make in the classroom—what we do with our students—can impact their lives."

"I really believe that projects *enhance* teaching and *enable* us to meet some of the challenges we are concerned about."

IDENTIFYING THE MAJOR CHALLENGES

During the year following the NAEYC conference, teachers, consultants, administrators, and teacher trainers continued to discuss the challenges they face in early childhood education and the role projects can play in meeting these challenges. All of these educators confront the same challenges that others involved in typical American early childhood centers and primary schools must deal with today. They do not work in ideal laboratory schools or centers in affluent communities, where children are coming to school with extensive backgrounds of traditional, school-related experiences. The communities where these educators work, and where children are growing up, have justifiable concerns about literacy—learning to read has become a struggle for many children. They, like many other teachers and administrators, have concerns about reading failure and how it leads to children feeling alienated from school and, eventually, dropping out of school. They are also trying to find successful strategies to help children struggling to learn a second language and the increasing number of children with special needs. The children and families most of these educators work with also face the problems associated with living in poverty. In addition, besides being concerned about how to provide the best educational experiences they can for their students, these teachers are experiencing an increasing emphasis on standards and assessment. During the year-long conversations, teachers and administrators identified five major challenges, which are discussed below.

Overcoming the Ill Effects of Poverty

The United States is an affluent nation; however, not all children enjoy abundant lives. The child poverty rate in the United States is substantially higher—often two to three times higher—than that of most other major, Western, industrialized nations (*Child Poverty Fact Sheet*, 2001). In 2000, 12.4 million children—more than one in six (17.5%)—nationwide lived below the poverty line (*Census 2000 Supplementary Survey*). The poverty rate was highest among young children: one in five (19.7%) five-year-olds were poor according to the 2000 census.

Children living in poverty are not spread evenly throughout our schools and early childhood centers. Some teachers have a significant number of poor children in their classrooms, while others have just one or two. Because poor families tend to live in certain areas of cities and towns, many schools or early childhood centers serve predominantly children living in poverty.

Consequently, a teacher may have a classroom containing children with inadequate health care, who are hungry, whose parents did not have favorable experiences with schools, who enter school with language delays, and/or who are more likely to have academic difficulties.

Moving Young Children Toward Literacy

Helping children learn to read is one of the most important tasks that early childhood teachers in our country face. Today, unlike in the past or in other societies, we want and expect all children to learn to read well.

> Academic success, as defined by high school graduation, can be predicted with reasonable accuracy by knowing someone's reading skill at the end of grade 3.... A person who is not at least a modestly skilled reader by the end of third grade is quite unlikely to graduate from high school. (Snow, Burns, & Griffin, 1998, p. 21)

Large numbers of school-age children, including children from all social classes, have significant difficulties in learning to read. Failure to learn to read adequately enough for continued school success is much more likely among children who are poor, nonwhite, and nonnative speakers of English (Snow et al., 1998). According to the National Report Card 2000, although the national average scale score has remained relatively stable for reading achievement, significant changes have occurred at the lower end of the performance distribution (Donahue et al., 2000). Scores at the 10th percentile in 2000 are significantly lower than in 1992. Thirty-seven percent of fourth graders failed to score at even the basic level. (Attaining the basic level means that when reading text appropriate for fourth graders, students are able to understand the overall meaning of what they read, make relatively obvious connections between the text and their own experiences, and extend the ideas in the text by making simple inferences.) The National Assessment Governing Board has set a goal that all students perform at the proficient level of reading.

Responding to Children's Special Needs

More and more children with special needs are being included in general preschool and child care programs. Seventy-five percent of the more than 5.5 million 6- through 21-year-olds with disabilities served under the Individuals with Disabilities Education Act (IDEA) in 1997–98 were educated in regular classrooms with their nondisabled peers (Department of Education, 2000).

When children with special needs are integrated into general education programs, all children can benefit. Some children with disabilities, however, require adjustment of the curriculum or classroom environment in order to be successful. To provide the necessary changes, teachers need up-to-date information on the specific special needs of each child and how to meet those needs.

In addition, children with special needs often require special support and services, and teachers are concerned about how these services will be provided for the children in their classrooms. Each child has unique needs that require commitment to provide the different supports needed for learning (Villa et al., 1995). In an early childhood environment, many special services are brought into the classroom. In some cases, additional staff are in the classroom with the teacher on a daily basis, which requires collaboration skills and flexibility. At other times, therapy or tutoring is needed, and the teacher must make room in the schedule for these activities.

Helping Children Learn a Second Language

The number of children learning a second language has grown significantly over the last decade. According to the 2000 census, 17.6% of the population over the age of five speaks a language other than English at home, in rural as well as urban areas. For example, in the small rural town of West Liberty, Iowa, 52% of the students in the elementary school are second-language learners. Throughout the United States, a variety of educational services are provided to second-language learners, including bilingual education, in which content instruction is provided in both English and the student's native language while the student develops proficiency in English; English as a second language (ESL), in which instruction is provided only in English; and dual-language programs, which provide instruction in both languages for all children in the classroom. It is not uncommon for a classroom to include children who speak several languages that the teacher is unable to understand.

Meeting Standards Effectively

The fifth and last challenge differs from the previous challenges because it focuses not on the needs of children and families but on the educational process. Out of concern that our educational system is not adequately preparing children, people are increasingly interested in monitoring what goes on in schools through standards and assessment. There is a collective concern that our educational system is failing children and families—that some children are not learning the skills they need to develop into productive, meaningful, and successful adults. Bringing education to the forefront of the national consciousness is appropriate and necessary. A nation cannot continue to be successful if its children do not possess the knowledge and skills necessary to be productive citizens. The nation's parents and schools need to be refocused on teaching and learning. However, the question is, What is the most effective way to refocus? The knowledge, skills, and dispositions that we want children to develop may be valid and worthwhile if they are culturally and geographically inclusive. The next step—How do we determine if children are developing the specified knowledge, skills, and dispositions?—is more complex. To be most effective, development must be monitored in the classroom as part of the teacher's responsibilities.

In summary, early childhood teachers have identified these tasks—these challenges—as consuming much of their day:

1. Overcoming the ill effects of poverty
2. Moving young children toward literacy
3. Responding to children's special needs
4. Helping children learn a second language
5. Meeting standards effectively

As the teachers expressed in the conversation in the van that opened this chapter, the project approach has provided them with a framework for using curriculum to help meet these challenges.

ADDITIONAL CONCERNS

The five challenges discussed above, however, are not the only sources of worry for early childhood educators. A number of educators at the NAEYC conference also discussed two additional issues that affect the growth and development of children and interfere with their ability to respond to educational experiences.

Television

Educators expressed concern about the dominant role that television plays in the lives of children. Although moderate and monitored television watching does not appear to impact children's development, many children in the United States watch a great deal of television—an average of four hours a day according to the American Academy of Pediatrics (2001). Extensive television watching negatively affects children's development, including decreasing school performance and increasing violent and aggressive behavior. Of special concern is heavy television watching during children's early years.

Quality Child Care

The wide variation in the quality of child care for children before they enter school and after-school care is also cause for concern among educators. Nonparental child care has been increasing, as the rate of employment of mothers outside the home has risen over the last decade. In the United States, 61% of infants, toddlers, and preschool children under the age of six are in child care (NAEYC, 1999). Forty-five percent of children under age one are in child care on a regular basis. According to the NAEYC (1999), both care and education programs may be inadequate.

> Recently research reports have found that for the most part, early care and education is only mediocre and many factors contribute to the lack of high-quality, affordable programs. The lack of adequate funding, especially for equitable compensation of early childhood professionals, is a core problem for many providers.

Quality programs that provide both care and education can be found in all types of early childhood settings. Children from these programs come into kindergarten with rich preschool experiences filled with stimulation—talking, interacting with adults, reading books, solving problems, and getting to know their world. The preschool experiences of other children, however, could be described as haphazard, inconsistent, and boring, thereby adding barriers to school success.

CHALLENGES, NOT DEFICITS

This book focuses on challenges that teachers in classrooms, on the front lines, are facing today. The def-

inition of challenge includes "a test of one's abilities or resources in a demanding but stimulating undertaking" (*American Heritage Dictionary of the English Language,* 2000, p. 308). Although some teachers feel overwhelmed by changes in the teaching environment, some also find their work to be interesting, enjoyable, and exciting as they are challenged to meet the needs of an increasingly diverse school population. In fact, some challenges that were the focus of the teachers' "Yes, but . . ." comments during the van ride have brought benefits to their classrooms and made teaching more fulfilling. The challenge of second-language learners and increasing language diversity, if it is embraced, results in all children and teachers learning more about other languages and cultures. Teachers are often fascinated as they observe children playing without the benefit of a common language; friendships develop, and eventually the second language begins to emerge. They often speak of feeling privileged to witness the emergence of a bilingual child, a goal that most teachers themselves have never achieved.

We have observed the same response to the inclusion of a child with special needs in the classroom. Children learn new social skills and develop empathy as they work and play daily in classrooms with children with special needs. Some of the teachers in this book also report that the incorporation of standards in their programs have brought a clarity to their teaching that had been lacking.

It is easy to get sidetracked by labels and categories, especially when an institution requires them in order to receive funding and support. It is important, however, that we understand the challenges we face. In *Star Teachers of Children in Poverty,* Martin Haberman (1995) discusses how educators should think about children living in poverty:

> How one approaches children at-risk is a critical point for discriminating among teachers and would be teachers and for predicting success in teaching children in poverty. Quitters and failures justify their lack of effectiveness by detailing inadequacies in the children. They frequently seem to want to know as much as possible about their children for the purpose of proving to themselves that teaching these children is impossible. Stars, on the other hand, learn about the children's lives for entirely different motives. They seek to become sensitive to the children's backgrounds because they genuinely care about them. . . . The critical distinction is whether they use this information to "prove" the children cannot be taught or to make their teaching more relevant. (p. 53)

In this book, we focus on challenges in order to help teachers break away from a deficit view of children and families. As teachers, we have pledged to support each child's development, no matter what his or her background is, and meet the educational needs of each individual child. Our children are our children, all of them.

THE IMPORTANCE OF RESILIENCY

One of the ways to help children facing difficulties in their lives is to provide experiences that build skills and attitudes essential to the development and maintenance of resiliency. Resiliency is the ability to recover from setbacks and maintain buoyancy. Some individuals who encounter difficulties in their lives are incapacitated by them, while others facing the same problems may overcome them and even become stronger and more motivated because of the experience. Because the challenges and concerns identified in this book continue outside of the school day, teachers can contribute to children's success by learning about and teaching resiliency skills and attitudes.

Studies of children who demonstrate resilience are useful for determining the skills and attitudes that contribute to a resilient personality. Garmezy (1983) identified common characteristics of successful students in high-poverty areas: good social skills, positive peer interactions, a high degree of social responsiveness and sensitivity, intelligence, empathy, a sense of humor, and critical problem-solving skills. Educators can help children develop these skills and attitudes—which will sustain them in difficult circumstances—through teacher-student interactions and how the classroom environment is structured.

According to Grotberg (1995), adults can support children's resiliency by providing opportunities to develop trust, autonomy, initiative, industry, and identity. These five building blocks of resiliency contribute to the ability to face, overcome, be strengthened by, or even be transformed by experiences of adversity (Grotberg, 1995).

Another way to think about resiliency is to focus on the development of self-esteem and self-efficacy. Winfield (1999) emphasizes the importance of establishing and maintaining self-esteem and self-efficacy as a way to foster resiliency. These skills are learned through interactions with peers and adults and successful accomplishments; "It is not learned in a decontextualized manner. It is not learned by completing a series of lessons in commercially available programs" (Winfield, 1999, p. 42). Self-efficacy develops when students learn that they have some control over certain things in their environments and that they are not helpless. In the early years, children are likely to develop self-efficacy when they have opportunities to solve problems and

reach goals, and they develop self-esteem when they see evidence of their learning and the positive reactions of adults to these successes.

Project work provides opportunities to build resiliency skills and attitudes. When children investigate topics of interest to them, they learn what it feels like to satisfy their own curiosity. They learn how to ask questions, identify adults who can give them information, and use resources. When children represent what they have learned by making a play environment, such as a hospital or grocery store or hosting an open house, they solve problems and learn to work with others to find solutions. Most important for resiliency, however, is the development of confidence in their own ability to make things happen.

THE ROLE OF CURRICULUM IN MEETING CHALLENGES

Experts have suggested a variety of solutions to the challenges faced by today's educators, including comprehensive early childhood programs with parent education and health components, community efforts to reduce poverty and violence, and collaboration to develop bilingual language programs. High-quality, comprehensive early childhood programs for children in poverty have been shown to result in long-term positive effects (Barnett & Boocock, 1998a, 1998b; Ramey & Campbell, 1991; Weikart, Bond, & McNeil, 1978). Strong administrative support for teachers and learner-focused professional development programs have been shown to help with several of the other challenges mentioned above, such as meeting a child's special needs. To successfully meet any of the five challenges requires the collaboration of teachers, parents, administrators, and members of the community and a strong commitment of resources.

It would be foolhardy to think there is one simple solution. To truly overcome the ill effects of poverty, our society needs to reduce the number of children living in poverty, not create ways to cope with the results. When poverty creates homelessness and violence in communities, the impact on children and their school achievement cannot be "solved" by how a teacher organizes the classroom.

Contribution of Curriculum

However, what children do all day in classrooms with their teachers and other children can make a meaningful, significant contribution to their development and achievement in school. Children can be involved in challenging activities that have meaning and build knowledge and skills, or they can spend their time doing activities that are meaningless to them and destroy their interest in learning.

Lilian Katz tells this story (Helm, 2000). She was observing in a preschool classroom where children were gluing cotton balls on large paper cutouts of lambs. This activity had been introduced by the teacher for the month of March, based on the saying, "March comes in like a lion and goes out like a lamb." When Katz asked the children why they were gluing cotton balls onto a cutout of a lamb, most of them did not have a clue. Finally, one little boy said, "I know! It is because lambs like to march!" His remark reveals that this activity had little meaning for the children and did little to build their skills or confidence.

Contrast that learning experience with Rebecca Wilson's description of a project on a combine harvester in her dual-language classroom:

> By generating their own questions, children took ownership in their project work on the combine. Throughout the project, our class was constantly asking questions. Mr. Danner took the time to answer the children's questions during our field site visit. Christian was curious about how many pieces were on the front part of the combine. He counted the corn headers and wrote down the numerals to find the answer. McKayla's question was, "Where do you make the wheel for a tractor?" She asked this question of an employee from H.D. Cline and remembered it all by herself. I wrote down his answer, "It comes from a store, and we bring them here to put them on tractors." McKayla was very intent upon copying down the answer and drawing it out. (Wilson, 2001)

The curriculum decisions that teachers make determine the daily experiences of children. Curriculum can be defined as *an organized framework that delineates the skills and content that children are to learn*. It includes the processes through which curricular goals are achieved, what teachers are expected to do to help children reach these goals, and the context in which teaching and learning occurs (Bredekamp & Rosegrant, 1995). Through decisions about curriculum, teachers can contribute toward meeting the challenges. Haberman (1995) describes the importance of the focus on curriculum.

> Essentially stars say, "Look, I have the most control over what and how I teach. I should be able to find a way to involve my children in learning, no matter what their out-of-school lives are like. That's my job, and that's what I work at until I find activities and projects that work— that turn them on to learning." (pp. 52–53)

The challenges we have been discussing can all be addressed through curriculum decisions. Although we specifically identify these challenges, we strongly caution against an interpretation of our work as a call for a separate curriculum for children who are living in poverty, learning a second language, and so forth. In making curriculum recommendations in this book, we do not and will not "prescribe" specific strategies for different kinds of children.

Curriculum Guidelines

The curriculum guidelines we provide for teachers who are facing these major challenges also can be used by educators not facing the specific challenges we have identified. The guidelines listed below are a composite of recommendations for best practices from a variety of researchers, theorists, and teachers in the field (Bowman, Donovan, & Burns, 2000; Bredekamp & Copple, 1997; DeVries, Reese-Learned, & Morgan, 1991; Katz, 1999; Katz & Chard, 1989; Neuman, Copple, & Bredekamp, 2000).

1. Curriculum should be engaging, interesting, and contribute to children's intellectual development (children learn to think by thinking).
2. Curriculum should incorporate both formal learning, through direct teacher instruction that is organized and consistent, and informal learning, in which children learn through interactions with the materials, the teacher, other children, and adults. (The younger the child, the more time is needed in informal experiences. It is important for children of five and six, however, to have systematic instruction in skills such as reading, writing, and numeracy.)
3. Curriculum should be focused on topics of study that are worth the time spent studying them, relevant to children's cultures, and related to the overall goals of children's education.
4. Curriculum should provide opportunities for children to integrate content and skills. (Informal experiences provide a context to practice and perfect skills that are introduced in the more formal curriculum.)
5. Curriculum should provide opportunities for children to take control of their learning, take the initiative, and find out that they are competent learners.
6. Curriculum should provide opportunities for children to try, and if they fail, to develop persistence in seeking solutions. This supports the development of resiliency.
7. Curriculum should be consistent with the age level of the child. For young children, this means experiences should be predominantly concrete, hands-on, and sensory. Children also should have an

opportunity to observe adults demonstrate and model processes and skills.

8. Curriculum should be language and literacy rich, including many relevant opportunities to talk, listen, and ask questions; to be read to, to read, and to use books for research; and to write.

9. Curriculum should be thought provoking and incorporate many opportunities for children to do scientific and mathematical thinking, including using numbers and counting to solve problems, observing living things and scientific processes, and conducting simple experiments and collecting data.

10. Curriculum should occur in the context of a caring community—a community that gives students a sense of physical and emotional safety and belonging, promotes cooperation, and celebrates successes.

11. Curriculum should provide opportunities for parents to participate, to strengthen the ties between parent and child, to enable parents to see school as relevant, and for the parent to see the child as a competent learner.

12. A curriculum and assessment plan with clearly delineated goals and a system of observing and collecting children's work should provide a framework for teacher decision making.

THE PROJECT APPROACH

One way, but by no means the only way, to provide the kind of curriculum described above is through the use of projects in early childhood education. Although the word *project* has many meanings in education, in this book we are following the definition provided by Lilian Katz (1994):

> A project is an in-depth investigation of a topic worth learning more about. The investigation is usually undertaken by a small group of children within a class, sometimes by a whole class, and occasionally by an individual child. The key feature of a project is that it is a research effort deliberately focused on finding answers to questions about a topic posed either by the children, the teacher, or the teacher working with the children. (p. 1)

The use of projects in early childhood curriculum is described in depth in *Young Investigators: The Project Approach in the Early Years* (Helm & Katz, 2001). In *The Power of Projects*, we move beyond an explanation of the project approach to explore how early childhood professionals can use project work to meet the challenges they encounter in their classrooms.

We are not suggesting that projects should make up the entire early childhood curriculum. Projects are only one kind of learning experience that children need. Teachers who use the project approach often also teach single concepts and utilize units, themes, and directed inquiry; they provide direct instruction regarding some academic skills, such as how to count or write a letter. They may organize experiences around a theme, a broad concept, or a topic like "seasons" or "animals" (Helm & Katz, 2001). When using a theme, teachers assemble books, photographs, and other materials related to it. Projects, where children decide what to investigate and what they want to know, often develop out of teacher-planned theme experiences.

Many preschool and kindergarten teachers also organize learning experiences around centers in the classroom. Materials and equipment for each area are selected to teach concepts and provide practice in skills that the teacher wishes the children to develop. Centers, such as a science corner, often provide background knowledge for children, allowing them to learn what interests them and gain familiarity with a topic so that they can think of meaningful questions.

Themes, units, learning centers, and direct instruction all have important places in early childhood curriculum. Some of the curriculum guidelines listed above, however, are more easily incorporated when children ask their own questions, conduct their own investigations, and make decisions about their activities. Projects provide contexts in which children's curiosity can be expressed purposefully and enable them to experience the joy of self-motivated learning. Well-developed projects engage children's minds and emotions and become adventures that teachers and children embark upon together.

The use of the project approach in the United States has been stimulated by information about projects developed in the preschools of Reggio Emilia, Italy. We have learned much from reading about and visiting Reggio Emilia and studying documentation of Reggio projects. We have found that the challenges faced in U.S. schools, however, differ greatly from challenges faced by early childhood teachers in Reggio Emilia, where there is little poverty and academic standards and assessment are not specified for preschools. We believe that engaging projects, as defined by the project approach (Helm & Katz, 2001; Katz & Chard, 1989), are especially meaningful for children growing up in poverty, learning a second language, and with special needs. We also believe that projects provide an excellent vehicle for moving children toward literacy and for accomplishing specific outcomes, such as those listed in most standards for early childhood education.

ORGANIZATION OF THE BOOK

The implications of using the project approach to meet challenges in early childhood classrooms are examined further by Lilian Katz in Chapter 2. She explores the contributions project work in the early years can make to intellectual development and later school achievement and how learning experiences can impact children at risk.

Chapters 3–7 each focus on one of the five major challenges identified above. The chapters are organized into three parts, the first of which provides information on the nature and extent of the particular challenge. In the second part, early childhood professionals who are using the project approach in their classrooms share their practical strategies for meeting the specific challenge. The strategies they list are then highlighted and illustrated in the third section, in which the teacher-authors describe how a project in their classrooms helped them meet the challenges.

The schools and centers represented in Chapters 3–7 include the following:

- An at-risk prekindergarten classroom in an urban elementary school
- A comprehensive, urban, early childhood program, with children ages six weeks through first grade, collaboratively funded by Head Start, the city school district, and a state prekindergarten program for children at risk
- A preschool program sponsored by a special education agency
- A dual-language kindergarten classroom
- A child care center where children's attendance is based on parental child care needs

In three of the programs, a majority of the children are racial/ethnic minorities. None of the programs have fewer than 30% of the children living in poverty, and in two, over 75% live in poverty. Children engaging in the projects described in Chapters 3–7 range in age from three years through first grade.

The issue of accountability is addressed in Chapter 8 through an expanded discussion of the role of teacher reflective practice and documentation, which are introduced in earlier chapters. Chapter 9 looks to the future. In Appendix A, teachers, administrators, and educational consultants discuss some questions and concerns frequently encountered when teachers begin to use the project approach to meet challenges. Appendix B includes an annotated list of recommended resources on the project approach.

This book shares the work of teachers who are using the project approach in their classrooms as a way to meet challenges. It was written not only to share but also to explore the use of the project approach. If the project approach is a good method for overcoming these challenges, are we getting the maximum benefit we can from using it? As we attempt to meet the challenges that face educator's in today's schools, we need to be willing to try new methods and to alter the ones already in use to meet the changing needs of our children. We invite teachers to try the practical strategies discussed here not only in project work but also in other learning experiences in their classrooms. Then we ask teachers to think of their own practical strategies to maximize project work and share it with others.

REFERENCES

American Academy of Pediatrics. (2001). *Policy statement: Children, adolescents, and television.* Elk Grove, IL: American Academy of Pediatrics.

American heritage dictionary of the English language (4th ed.). (2000). Boston: Houghton Mifflin.

Barnett, W. S., & Boocock, S. S. (Eds.). (1998a). *Early care and education for children in poverty: Promises, programs, and long-term results.* Albany: State University of New York Press.

Barnett, W. S., & Boocock, S. S. (Eds.). (1998b). *Long-term effects on cognitive development and school success.* Albany: State University of New York Press.

Bowman, B. T., Donovan, M. S., & Burns, M. S. (Eds.). (2000). *Eager to learn.* Washington, DC: National Academy Press.

Bredekamp, S., & Copple, C. (Eds.). (1997). *Developmentally appropriate practice in early childhood programs* (Rev. ed.). Washington DC: National Association for the Education of Young Children.

Bredekamp, S., & Rosegrant, T. (1995). *Reaching potentials: Transforming early childhood curriculum and assessment* (Vol. 2). Washington, DC: National Association for the Education of Young Children.

Census 2000 supplementary survey. Washington DC: U.S. Census Bureau.

Child poverty fact sheet. (2001, June). New York: National Center for Children in Poverty, Columbia University.

Department of Education, U.S. (2000). *Twenty-second annual report to Congress on the implementation of the Individuals with Disabilities Education Act.* Washington, DC: U.S. Department of Education.

DeVries, R., Reese-Learned, H., & Morgan, P. (1991). Sociomoral development in direct-instruction, eclectic and constructivist kindergartens: A study of children's enacted interpersonal understandings. *Early Childhood Research & Practice, 6*(4), 473–517.

Donahue, P. L., Finnegan, R. J., Lutkus, A. D., Allen, N. L., & Campbell, J. R. (2000). *The nation's report card: Fourth grade reading 2000* (NCES 2001499). Washington DC: National Center for Education Statistics.

Garmezy, N. (1983). Stressors of childhood. In N. Garmezy & M. Rutter (Eds.), *Stress, coping and development in children* (pp. 43–84). New York: McGraw-Hill.

Grotberg, E. H. (1995). *A guide to promoting resilience in children: Strengthening the human spirit.* The Hague, The Netherlands: Bernard Van Leer Foundation.

Haberman, M. (1995). *Star teachers of children in poverty.* West Lafayette, IN: Kappa Delta Pi.

Helm, J. H. (2000). *Gifts from Lilian Katz: Stories, anecdotes and profound thoughts.* Springfield, IL: Illinois Association for the Education of Young Children.

Helm, J. H., and Katz, L. G. (2001). *Young Investigators: The Project Approach in the Early Years.* New York: Teachers College Press.

Katz, L. G. (1994). *The project approach.* Champaign, IL: ERIC Clearinghouse on Elementary and Early Childhood Education.

Katz, L. G. (1999, November 18). *Current perspectives on education in the early years: Challenges for the new millennium.* Paper presented at the Ninth Annual Rudolph Goodridge Memorial Lecture, Barbados, West Indies.

Katz, L. G., & Chard, S. C. (1989). *Engaging children's minds: The project approach.* Greenwich, CT: Ablex Publishing Corporation.

National Association for the Education of Young Children (NAEYC). (1999). *The care and education of young children in the United States* [Website]. Retrieved 2001 from www. naeyc.org.

Neuman, S. B., Copple, C., & Bredekamp, S. (2000). *Learning to read and write: Developmentally appropriate practices for young children.* Washington, DC: National Association for the Education of Young Children.

Ramey, C. T., & Campbell, F. A. (1991). Poverty, early-childhood education, and academic competence: The Abcedarian Experiment. In A. Huston (Ed.), *Children reared in poverty* (pp. 190–221). New York: Cambridge University Press.

Snow, C. E., Burns, M. S., & Griffin, P. (Eds.). (1998). *Preventing reading difficulties in young children.* Washington, DC: National Academy Press.

Villa, R. A., Klift, E. V. D., Udis, J., Thousand, J. S., Nevin, A. I., Kunc, N., & Chapple, J. W. (1995). Questions, concerns, beliefs, and practical advice about inclusive environments. In R. A. Villa & J. S. Thousand (Eds.), *Creating an inclusive school* (pp. 136–61). Alexandria, VA: Association for Supervision and Curriculum Development.

Weikart, D. P., Bond, J. T., & McNeil, J. T. (1978). *The Ypsilanti Perry Preschool project: Preschool years and longitudinal results through fourth grade.* Ypsilanti, MI: High/Scope Press.

Wilson, R. (2001). The combine project: An experience in a dual language classroom [Electronic version]. *Early Childhood Research & Practice, 3*(1).

Winfield, L. F. (1999). Developing resilience in urban youth. In B. Cessarone (Ed.), *Resilience guide: A collection of resources on resilience in children and families.* Champaign, IL: ERIC Clearinghouse on Elementary and Early Childhood Education.

CHAPTER 2

Building a Good Foundation for Children

Lilian G. Katz

In the previous chapter, Judy Harris Helm defined five major challenges confronting educators of young children. Some teachers must cope with all five challenges simultaneously; others may have to focus more on one than others. Whatever the case may be, teachers can respond to the challenges and at the same time help set the foundations for children's futures by incorporating good project work into the early childhood curriculum.

When thinking about the design of early childhood education that will set a good foundation for the future, it may be helpful to compare how architects, engineers, and builders approach the design of a foundation for a building. At the outset, three basic principles must be applied to the design of the building's foundation. The first principle is to *base the design on comprehensive information concerning the nature of the ground* the structure will be resting upon; the structure is designed differently depending on whether the ground is rock, mud, or sandy soil. All available information about the ground is carefully considered during the design process. In a similar way, a teacher gathers as much information as possible about the kinds of experiences that each child in the group has or has not already had and what each child has or has not already learned. A teacher uses this information to determine the experiences that should be offered to the children. In order to do this effectively, the teacher devotes time and effort not only to knowing *about* each child but also to *knowing* each child.

The second principle of foundation design *is to focus on the characteristics of the structure* that is being built. Information about the building's attributes, such as its height, weight, area, horizontal expanse, and so forth, is taken into account. Similarly, curriculum developers and teachers plan experiences for young children in terms of their broad aims and goals as well as their more immediate specific objectives. A good foundation in the early years then, takes into account all domains of development—social, emotional, cognitive, physical, aesthetic, cultural, and other fundamental aspects of growth, development, and learning; solid early childhood education is not simply limited to learning a few letters of the alphabet and mastery of a few discrete skills practiced on work sheets. Rather, the experiences educators expose their students to are based on the part they can be expected to play as a foundation for children's future learning and on the best available knowledge of the relationships between early experience and mature functioning. An essential feature of good project work is that it provides children with contexts in which they are motivated to ask for help in the use of basic skills (e.g., writing captions for drawings or bar graphs) as they work with purpose to represent the findings of their investigations.

Finally, the third basic principle of designing foundations is *to anticipate all of the possible stresses* the structure is likely to be subjected to in the future; these might include hurricane-force winds, tornadoes, heavy loads of snow, floods, earthquakes, and the like. Likewise, curriculum developers and teachers strive to lay foundations that can support long-term goals, such as the fundamental goal of all education: developing and supporting a robust disposition to continue learning for a lifetime rather than just focusing on short-term gains on annual tests.

Educators might also keep in mind what builders know only too well: if the foundation of a building is not properly laid at the outset, it can be difficult and expensive to repair later; indeed, some kinds of early errors may even cause significant injuries in the future.

Architects have extensive data from experience and research on the relationship between foundations and stress resistance. One of the most intractable issues in the field of early education and child development, however, is that the connection between early experiences and long-term stress management is difficult to pin down. Donaldson (1978) pointed out long ago that during the first few years of school, most children "seem eager, lively [and] happy . . . the problem then is to understand how something that begins so well can often end so badly" (p. 13). There are many possible reasons for the gradual and widespread disaffection with school in the United States (Osborn, 1997). In other words, determining what is the best foundation for the complex structures being built is much more difficult for educators than for builders. However, our experiences of working with teachers who adopt the project approach, as described in the following chapters, suggest that the inclusion of *good* project work in the early years—indeed, throughout the elementary school period—can address all three principles of laying a good foundation.

PRINCIPLE ONE: GATHER INFORMATION

A project is defined as children undertaking an extended in-depth investigation of events or phenomena worth learning more about within their own environment. As already discussed above, the first principle of building foundations is to design it on the basis of the extensive information gathered about the ground. When launching a project, the teacher focuses on each of the children and the experiences, knowledge, skills, and interests each bring to the topic. The teacher considers the variety of interests in the group; the potential value learning about a particular topic might afford for various individuals and the group as a whole; the local resources readily available; and how the topic might fit into the state or local standards. With this information, the teacher takes the final responsibility for selecting the topic to be investigated in a project (see Katz & Chard, 1998).

Any group of young children in a preschool, child care, or kindergarten setting will invariably have had diverse experiences; acquired a range of knowledge, skills, and abilities; and have varied interests. In the case of children from low socioeconomic status (SES) families, many will have had little exposure to books; being read to; or being encouraged to write words, read signs, and other school-related activities. All children, however, have a range of experiences particular to their environments. For example, they have experienced various foods and eating places, kinds of transportation,

shops and stores, kinds of residences and neighborhoods, and perhaps a school bus (see Harkema, 1999). All of these variations are easily addressed in the course of good project work.

Project work is usually organized in three sequential phases (see Figure 2.1). During the first phase, the teacher helps children clarify the focus of the project and the questions their investigation will answer. The children share their prior knowledge and experiences related to the topic in various ways. Thus, the teacher deepens his or her knowledge of each of the children and notes ways to support and strengthen their progress in all learning areas as the project proceeds.

During the second phase of project work, the children, usually working in small groups on subtopics related to the main topic under investigation, take initiative and responsibility for data gathering. Depending on the ages of the children and the nature of the topic, this phase will involve the children visiting a field site and interviewing people who can answer their questions. They record and share the ideas and information emerging from their observations and research through such activities as making constructions and drawing charts indicating measurements of relevant phenomena.

In the third phase, with the guidance of the teacher, the children plan and conduct a culminating activity through which the story of the investigation and its findings are summarized and shared. Throughout this process, the teacher has ample opportunity to note the progress of each child and to encourage and support further learning based on teacher observations.

PRINCIPLE TWO: CONSIDER THE LONG-TERM EFFECTS OF EXPERIENCES ON CHILDREN'S EDUCATION

The second principle of designing foundations is to ensure its long-term viability by considering the characteristics of the building that will eventually rest on top of it. In planning experiences for young children, teachers must focus on the broad aims and goals of education as well as the more immediate specific objectives. In our view, one of the long-term goals of early education is to strengthen and support children's inborn tendencies to be curious and deeply engaged in making the best sense they can of their experiences. One of the important features of good project work is that throughout an investigation the children can express curiosity and engagement by being encouraged to take initiative and responsibility for what is accomplished. The role of the children is both interactive and active, not only in the pursuit of information, but also

Figure 2.1 Using the project approach in the early years.

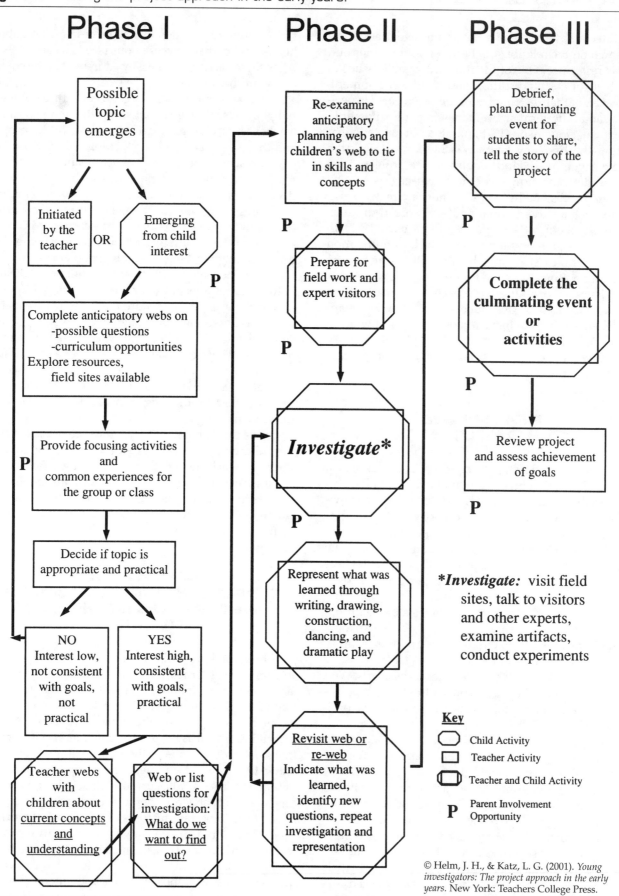

Phase I

Possible topic emerges

Initiated by the teacher OR Emerging from child interest

P

Complete anticipatory webs on
-possible questions
-curriculum opportunities
Explore resources,
field sites available

P Provide focusing activities
and
common experiences for
the group or class

Decide if topic is
appropriate and practical

NO
Interest low,
not consistent
with goals,
not
practical

YES
Interest high,
consistent
with goals,
practical

Teacher webs
with
children about
<u>current concepts
and
understanding</u>

Web or list
questions for
investigation:
<u>What do we
want to find
out?</u>

Phase II

Re-examine anticipatory planning web and children's web to tie in skills and concepts

P

Prepare for
field work and
expert visitors

P

*Investigate**

P

Represent what was
learned through
writing, drawing,
construction,
dancing, and
dramatic play

<u>Revisit web or
re-web</u>
Indicate what was
learned,
identify new
questions, repeat
investigation and
representation

Phase III

Debrief,
plan culminating
event for
students to share,
tell the story of the
project

P

**Complete the
culminating event
or
activities**

P

Review project
and assess achievement
of goals

P

Investigate: visit field
sites, talk to visitors
and other experts,
examine artifacts,
conduct experiments

<u>Key</u>

⬭ Child Activity

☐ Teacher Activity

▱ Teacher and Child Activity

P Parent Involvement
Opportunity

© Helm, J. H., & Katz, L. G. (2001). *Young
investigators: The project approach in the early
years.* New York: Teachers College Press.

in representing and sharing the information gained. In addition, the teacher encourages the children to inspect their own work and joint efforts in terms of whether the outcomes correspond to their intentions and how the work accomplished so far might be improved, added to, or otherwise changed.

By contrast, during traditional formal academic instruction, the role of children is more passive, reactive, and receptive. While a passive role can be appropriate for some of the children's experiences in the early years, the curriculum should be balanced so that frequent daily opportunities to make decisions and choices support and strengthen vital intellectual dispositions and minimize the extent to which children become restless or bored during their time in the class or program. Sooner or later the novelty of coloring work sheets wears off; the powerful inborn dispositions to learn, explore, and make sense of experiences may be weakened or damaged in many children after a few years of such passive, receptive instructional experiences.

There is now an impressive body of evidence indicating that early, formal, didactic instruction in basic academic skills, when compared to curriculum approaches that offer greater opportunity for children to take initiative (as described in Chapters 3–7), *may* produce more positive results on standardized measures *in the short term, but not for school-related achievement in the long term* (see, for example, Golbeck, 2001; Marcon, 1995, 2000). The differential short- versus long-term effects are difficult to interpret. The most likely explanation is that after a period of formal instruction becomes boring to young children, they may be physically present in the class but may drop out psychologically.

There are also data showing that excessive formal academic instruction in the early years has greater damaging long-term effects for boys than for girls (Marcon, 1992, 1995, 2000; Miller & Bizzell, 1983). Marcon (2000), in summarizing her long-term, follow-up data comparing the effects of curricula that are academically directed versus those that are child-initiated, states that

> In general, boys do not adjust as well as do girls to didactic early learning approaches. Boys show more stress behaviors in DIP [developmentally inappropriate practice] kindergartens. This is especially true for African American boys of lower socioeconomic status. Development and achievement of inner-city boys are fostered by kindergartens that emphasize socio-emotional growth over academics and are hindered by overly academic, didactic kindergarten experiences. (p. 359)

This gender effect is difficult to interpret. One contributing factor is very likely the well-established gender differences in neurological and linguistic development that put girls ahead of boys during the early years (Maccoby, 1998). An even more powerful factor may be that the passive-receptive role imposed by formal academic instruction is more difficult for boys to adapt to than for girls. On the basis of an extensive in-depth review of the research, Maccoby (1998) points out that boys, more so than girls, engage in "ego displays," in which they vie for status and engage in competitive and risk-taking behavior and strive for dominance (p. 57). Boys attempt to be active agents of affairs more than girls, who are socialized to accept a passive or submissive role more easily. Furthermore, boys' resistance to and discomfort with the passive role may be greater in some cultures or subcultures than others; for example, boys raised in cultures in which males are expected to be more dominant experience a discontinuity between their home culture and the culture of school. In addition, such gender-related role preferences may be even more differentiated by socioeconomic status within cultures and subcultures, creating an additional challenge to teachers who work with children of low-SES families.

In the course of good projects, boys and girls working in small groups are encouraged and expected to make decisions about how to proceed with data gathering and how to share responsibility for the work. They are encouraged to argue and work together to arrive at the best possible solutions to their differences. The teacher meets with the small groups as needed to offer support and suggestions, convey expectations that the group will proceed with the work, and note the progress of individual children in all areas of development.

Literacy

Extensive research on issues related to the development of literacy indicates that low-SES families provide less verbal interaction; thus, the vocabulary of these children is much more limited than that of higher-SES children. Furthermore, vocabulary size has been shown to influence the development of literacy skills.

The emphasis on formal academic instruction in preschool programs for children of low-SES families is often justified on the basis of their need to "catch up" with their more advantaged peers. Some observers of the SES differences assert that less-advantaged children do not have "time to waste" on play and the like. As indicated in the National Academy of Sciences report *Eager to Learn*, however, the potential for preschools to provide opportunities for children from low-SES groups to develop skills they might not otherwise acquire will be realized *only* if these programs provide the quality of learning experiences to which children in higher-SES groups are exposed (Bowman, Donovan, & Burns, 2001).

The children of high-SES families usually do not get their start on early literacy by being drilled in large groups on letters of the alphabet or meaningless phonemes practiced out of context. These children are often read to, encouraged to try to make out meaningful words and signs, and develop comparatively rich vocabularies in the course of conversations with adults about events and phenomena in context. In addition, higher-SES children observe adults around them in the act of reading more often than low-SES children. Our work has shown that low-SES children are helped more when they are encouraged to deeply engage in research on phenomena that are meaningful to them; it is clear to them that their own firsthand experiences and insights are respected; and their suggestions for how to proceed with the investigations are solicited and adopted. Expecting low-SES children to "catch up" with their more privileged peers by daily submitting them to long periods of passive instruction on discrete bits of information and skills, the purposes of which are, at best, obscure to them, may cause them to appear to be "caught up" in the short term. The long-term adequacy of such a foundation, however, is not supported by current data.

This is not to say, however, that all reading instruction should occur only within the context of more informal curriculum such as project work. When children reach the age at which the mastery of reading is reasonable—around six years old—more formal instruction in reading can be helpful. For low-SES children, this instruction is best when it occurs on a regular basis alongside interactive and active experiences such as project work.

Another consideration in building a solid foundation for the long-term goal of literacy is the importance of good communicative and linguistic experiences early on in education. Project work can help provide these experiences by allowing frequent and rich opportunities for meaningful conversations as children share their ideas, raise questions, offer suggestions to each other, conduct interviews, question visiting experts, and argue about various aspects of the work. By emphasizing the role of communicative competence in literacy acquisition, educators take into account that children and the adults who work with them *must have something of interest to communicate about*—something that matters, is important, and is meaningful to them. Extensive experience of working with early childhood teachers as they implement the project approach indicates that even at the preschool level, children often spontaneously ask their teachers for help in how to write things down. In many other countries, children are not taught to read but instead are introduced to literacy by writing (e.g., Sweden and Italy)—a process in which children are in an active rather than passive role.

Their motive to communicate in a wide variety of media is strengthened because the meaning and purposes are clear to them (see Beneke, 1998). Adults often underestimate how deeply and seriously involved even young children can become in investigations of things around them; they do not have to have "fun" with the work, but they do need to experience satisfaction from persistence, solving puzzles, checking predictions, and communicating their views to others. In project work, the children are under no pressure to compete with classmates for scores and grades. Their motivation is genuine communication with others about what they have found out and how they can synthesize, summarize, and share the information. As Stipek and Greene (2001) point out:

> Studies of classroom environments suggest that didactic and performance-oriented instruction, in which information about relative performance is salient, combined with low levels of nurturing and responsiveness to children can depress preschoolers' and kindergartners' motivation. (p. 82)

During the second, and part of the third, phases of project work, the small groups who have studied particular subtopics are expected to develop a report of their findings to entire class. The teacher is available for consultation as the need arises. When the teacher is not available to offer immediate guidance, he or she can suggest that those with questions turn to other classmates who are likely to have the knowledge and skills that would be helpful. The preparation and presentation of these reports provide meaningful and purposeful effort and motivation to communicate effectively with others. If all the children in a class study the same details and the same topics at the same time, they have no such genuine reason or purpose to present their new knowledge or communicate their experiences to each other. In this and many other respects, project work is full of meaning to the children and can be deeply engaging. The children are motivated to address questions they have posed rather than to satisfy their teachers' demands for the correct answers.

Sharing Responsibility

Of course, not all topics are equally interesting to every child in a group. For those who might be more interested in a different topic, the teacher can acknowledge the feeling by saying something like "I understand that you are not especially interested in the Bike Shop Project. I hope the next project we do will be more interesting for you. In the meantime, do what you can to help the others in your group." In this way, the teacher expresses genuine understanding and respect

Figure 2.2 A prediction table developed during the first phase of a project on a bicycle shop.

Question	Predictions	Findings
How do you fix flat tires?	Use Band-Aids Put a patch on the hole Pump it with air	
How do the spokes stay in the wheel?	They use a special glue	
What does a racer cost?	Ten dollars A thousand dollars	

for the child and makes clear the importance of working and helping others, even when a child is not deeply interested in the activity. Young children do not have to like everything they are required to do in school, but it is important for their disinterest to be understood and accepted, even if it cannot be acted upon. Thus, the disposition to participate, contribute, and share in the responsibility for the work of the group and one's larger community—even when the effort is not especially interesting—can be developed and strengthened and can serve as a foundation for our children's effective participation in a democracy for their whole lives.

The Disposition to be Reflective

During the final phase of a project, the teacher and children discuss plans for bringing the project to a close. The discussions include some debriefing concerning what has and has not been learned about the topic; they may also examine how the information that has been gathered compares to the children's predictions offered during the first phase of the project. For example, during the first phase of a preschool project on bicycles, the teacher can help the children to develop a chart as shown in Figure 2.2.

The children seek answers to the questions listed on the chart during the second phase. As the teacher guides the children in the creation of the chart, he or she can ask such questions as "What makes you think that the repairman uses Band-Aids?" The question is asked in such a way as to encourage children to develop the disposition to reflect on the bases of their own ideas, thus laying the foundation for a lifelong meta-cognitive habit. During the final phase of the project, the children discuss and summarize their findings and can deepen their appreciation for how much there is to learn about many ordinary things around them.

As the group develops plans for various culminating activities, such as an evening open house for their parents or reports and presentations of their work to other classes, the teacher encourages the children to think about which aspects of their experience and findings might be of greatest interest to their audience and should be included in their account of their experience. Provoking children to anticipate how others are likely to respond to their presentations and what others are likely to find interesting sets a foundation for the development of social cognitive skills, which they will employ throughout their lives.

Some children may make predictions or suggestions with which others will disagree. The teacher encourages the children to share their own reasoning about their proposals and guides them to make compromises and resolve conflicting opinions. Only three or four of the children in the group may engage in intense argument about what should be planned, but those children who are observing the progress of the arguments and their resolutions are also learning useful cognitive, linguistic, and social skills to apply on future occasions. This kind of provocation sets the foundation for supporting the development and strengthening of social cognitive capabilities, life skills that will serve the children for their entire futures.

PRINCIPLE THREE: ANTICIPATING FUTURE SOURCES OF STRESS

The third basic principle of designing foundations is to *anticipate all of the possible stresses* that the building will be subjected to, and then design it to be able to withstand them successfully. In a similar way, when planning experiences for children, the focus is on lifelong goals for each individual and not merely on grade-level test scores and achievement goals for the school years.

When planning to help children cope effectively with the stresses and demands they are likely to encounter in the future, teachers should keep in mind two important distinctions:

1. The distinction between having skills and knowledge and the disposition to use them
2. The distinction between academic and intellectual goals

Concerning the first of these, it is possible, for example, for young children to master basic literacy-related skills (e.g., phonics) and do fairly well on tests about them. But because the processes involved in the mastery of English-language phonics may be difficult for many children during the early years, they may fail to acquire a disposition to become readers. In other words, the children have reading skills—and, indeed, may perform fairly well on tests for which they have been prepared—however, the processes involved in learning the skills discourage the disposition to be a reader. A child with a robust disposition toward reading will continue to read and, thus, continue to develop and improve his or her reading ability. In this way, a middle-school child becomes a good reader and eventually can comprehend advanced-level texts. A child's enjoyment of reading can serve him or her in the future in relation to a very wide range of life's demands. Furthermore, the fundamental purpose of reading is comprehension, which is not improved by drill and practice and work sheets but by reading for knowledge, understanding, interest, and other purposes. When children have ample experiences of reading for purposes that are clear to them—as in the case of gathering data for a project—their dispositions to read can be strengthened.

Science offers another example of the distinction between skills and the dispositions to apply them. As the Committee on Developments in the Learning of Science states in its report,

> Children are both problem solvers and problem generators: children attempt to solve problems presented to them, and they also seek novel challenges. They refine and improve their problem-solving strategies not only in the face of failure, but also by building on prior success. They persist because success and understanding are motivating in their own right. (Bransford, Brown, & Cocking, 1999, p. 100)

The second distinction noted above—between academic and intellectual goals—is especially important during the early years. Young children arrive at their first school experience with powerful inborn intellectual dispositions—to make sense of experience and to learn, analyze, theorize, hypothesize, make predictions, and so forth. These tendencies are stronger in some children than in others. While intellectual goals are concerned with strengthening these inborn dispositions, academic goals address important skills and knowledge most young children need adult help to learn. Academic goals deal with relatively small and discrete elements such as phonics, conventions of spelling, the rules of punctuation, and so forth. While these elements must eventually be mastered, they are more likely to be so in the early years when their uses and functions are evident to the children, such as through project work.

Emphasis on strengthening intellectual desires is also recommended because the amount of knowledge and information that is available and being developed in the twenty-first century is so overwhelming that the disposition to go on learning throughout life seems to take on increasing importance. The issue has been stated as follows:

> The sheer magnitude of human knowledge renders its coverage by education an impossibility; rather, the goal of education is better conceived as helping students develop the intellectual tools and learning strategies needed to acquire the knowledge that allows people to think productively about history, science and technology, social phenomena, mathematics, and the arts. Fundamental understanding about subjects, including how to frame and ask meaningful questions about various subject areas . . . can assist them in becoming self-sustaining, lifelong learners. (Bransford, Brown, & Cocking, 1999, p. 5)

Deliberate and explicit attention to strengthening worthwhile dispositions in the early years is strongly recommended partly because resistant attitudes toward learning may become more difficult to change with increasing age. At the same time, desirable dispositions—particularly the intellectual ones—typically present at birth (e.g., the dispositions to be curious and become attached to caretakers) may be seriously weakened and even lost if not purposefully strengthened, and they may be very difficult to recover as a child grows older. Weak or poor foundations of education may make children vulnerable to misinformation, negative attitudes toward learning, and unpredictable sources of stress as they grow older. A foundation is far more likely to serve children well when they have frequent, firsthand experiences of using academic skills in the service of their intellectual dispositions. In precisely this way, good project work provides contexts, texts, and pretexts for young children to experience directly the purposes and uses of academic skills, such as the conventions of writing and ways of representing their observations using various mathematical processes.

It is unlikely, however, that positive feelings toward reading and education can be learned through instruc-

Figure 2.3 The goal of increasing the overlap of the quality of processes, products, and content in project work.

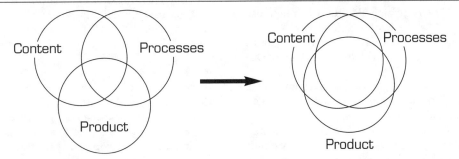

tion, exhortation, or indoctrination. Aside from the important dispositions that can be assumed to be present at birth (e.g., curiosity and desire to learn), others are likely to be learned from being around people who possess them and in whose behavior the dispositions can easily be observed by children. For example, a parent's disposition to be a reader can be fairly visible to a young child and therefore can be a source of modeling.

Furthermore, for dispositions to be strengthened, they must be manifested or practiced with some frequency. They must also be experienced as satisfying and effective rather than being met with rejection or criticism. Thus, a child who asks a teacher for clarification of something just presented and is answered with: "You should have been paying attention"—as sometimes happens to our children—is unlikely to have his or her disposition to raise questions and seek deeper understanding strengthened. Appropriate curricula and appropriate teaching methods should provide contexts and opportunities for children to manifest desirable dispositions, such as to investigate, hypothesize and make predictions, cooperate and collaborate with others, resolve cognitive conflicts, and test their hypotheses and predictions. These experiences are all part of good project work.

INTEGRATING THE PRINCIPLES FOR THE BEST FOUNDATION

When considered together, the principles outlined above imply another important way of responding to the challenges and laying the best possible foundation for future learning. Educators should strive to ensure that the three major elements of the curriculum are equally emphasized in terms of their quality: the *processes*, the *products*, and the *content* of the children's work.

As already indicated, there are many important processes included in good project work. For example, in support of children's intellectual development,

project work involves them in, among other activities, undertaking investigations, predicting answers and checking them, arguing with each other about the bases for their theories and predictions, and hypothesizing causes and effects. In support of their social development, project work involves children in cooperating with and assisting their peers, sharing responsibilities for what is accomplished, and similar purposeful acts of social interaction. While these processes are very important in the early years, project work also can stimulate children to develop their own criteria for assessing the products of their work, especially as they prepare to share their findings with others. For example, children can be encouraged to examine how they have represented their findings in murals, structures, bar graphs, photographs, and, with increasing age, how completely or accurately they have written their thoughts and ideas so that others can appreciate them.

While both the processes and products involved in project work present multiple opportunities to learn a wide variety of important skills, the nature of the content studied is equally important. It is not sufficient for children to be engaged in good processes that may or may not yield good products; they are most likely to experience maximum learning if these two elements of the curriculum are focused on the examination of worthwhile topics—topics that deepen the children's understanding of significant events and phenomena around them, where things come from, how they are made, and what goes on behind the scenes that are familiar to them (see Figure 2.3). Children will also learn to appreciate how others contribute to their well-being.

This chapter began with a discussion of three basic principles in the design of the foundations of strong structures. With the guidance of adults in the complex processes involved in good project work, a solid foundation can be available to children for their future learning.

REFERENCES

Beneke, S. (1998). *Rearview mirror: Reflections on a preschool car project* (ED 424 977). Champaign, IL: ERIC Clearinghouse on Elementary and Early Childhood Education.

Bowman, B. T., Donovan, M. S., & Burns, M. S. (Eds.). (2001). *Eager to learn: Educating our preschoolers.* Washington, DC: National Academy Press.

Bransford, J. D., Brown, A. L., & Cocking, R. R. (Eds). (1999). *How people learn: Brain, mind, experience, and school.* Washington, DC: National Academy Press.

Donaldson, M. (1978). *Children's minds.* Glasgow: Fontana.

Golbeck, S. L. (2001). Instructional models for early childhood: In search of a child-regulated/teacher-guided pedagogy. In S. Golbeck (Ed.), *Psychological perspectives on early childhood education: Reframing dilemmas in research and practice* (pp. 153–80). Mahwah, NJ: Erlbaum.

Harkema, R. (1999). The school bus project. *Early Childhood Research and Practice, 1*(2). Retrieved September 2002 from http://ecrp.uiuc.edu/v1n2/harkema.html

Katz, L. G., & Chard, S. C. (1998). *Issues in selecting topics for projects* (EDO-PPS.98-8).Champaign, IL: ERIC Clearinghouse on Elementary & Early Childhood Education.

Maccoby, E. (1998). *Growing up apart: Coming together.* Boston: Harvard University Press.

Marcon, R. A. (1992). Differential effects of three preschool models on inner-city 4-year-olds. *Early Childhood Research Quarterly, 7*(4), 517–30.

Marcon, R. (1995, May). Fourth-grade slump: The cause and cure. *Principal,* 17–20.

Marcon, R. (2000, April 16). *Impact of preschool models on educational transitions from early childhood to middle-childhood and into early adolescence.* Poster session at the Conference on Human Development, Memphis, TN.

Miller, L., & Bizzell, J. (1983). Long-term effects of four preschool programs. *Child Development, 54,* 727–41.

Osborn, J. W. (1997). Race and academic disidentification. *Journal of Educational Psychology, 89*(4), 728–35.

Stipek, D. J., & Greene, J. K. (2001). Achievement motivation in early childhood: Cause for concern or celebration? In S. Golbeck (Ed.), *Psychological perspectives on early childhood education: Reframing dilemmas in research and practice* (pp. 64–91). Mahwah, NJ: Erlbaum.

CHAPTER 3

Overcoming the Ill Effects of Poverty

Contributors: Judy Harris Helm and Jean Lang

DEFINING THE CHALLENGE
Judy Harris Helm

The impact of poverty can be pervasive. In 1999, according to the U.S. Census Bureau, a child was poor if the family's annual cash income was below $13,290 for a three-person family or $16,400 for a family of four. When incomes are this low, children are at greater risk of infant mortality and health problems that affect their growth and school achievement. Parenting and care giving may be disrupted. Stressed parents are often occupied with providing food, clothing, and shelter, so they have limited time or energy available for individual interactions with their children.

Poverty does not affect all children in the same way, and they are more at risk when poverty occurs early in their lives. Extreme poverty during the first five years of life has especially negative effects on a child's future compared to less extreme poverty experienced later in childhood. If a family lives in poverty for a limited time, the effects on children's development and school achievement are not as likely to be long term, as compared to children who live in persistent poverty throughout their childhoods. A child who lives in a less economically favored environment throughout his or her formative years will be at risk of not graduating from high school and achieving meaningful employment. The degree of impoverishment also reflects the degree of risk. Today, 7% of America's children overall and 8% of children under age six live in extreme poverty, that is, in families with incomes below 50% of the poverty line (*Child Poverty Fact Sheet*, 2001).

The effects of poverty on children's development and education includes decreased verbal ability and achievement (Duncan & Brooks-Gunn, 1997). Children from families with lower SES are more prone to reading difficulties and lower overall academic achievement than children from families with higher SES (Snow, Burns, & Griffin, 1998). Patterns of interaction, especially verbal interaction, between children and parents are significantly different in lower-income families (Hart & Risley, 1995). Hart and Risley (1995) conducted a study of the growth in language and interaction patterns of 42 children from birth through three years. They found that children in lower-income environments not only learn fewer words than children in more affluent families but also have fewer opportunities to practice those words in interactions. In the foreword to their book, Lois Bloom summarizes Hart and Risley's findings about the relationship between income and children's development:

> Why do children differ so drastically in the trajectories of their word learning? It turns out that *frequency matters*. The powerful lesson to be learned ... is that even though they have the *same* kinds of experiences with language and interactions in their home, children born into homes with fewer economic resources have fewer of these experiences. And the consequence is that they learn fewer words and acquire a vocabulary of words more slowly. (p. xi)

How significant is the difference? Hart and Risley's research found that by the time children were three years old, *parents* in low-SES families had fewer different words in their cumulative monthly vocabularies than did the *children* in high-SES families in the same period of time. Children living in poverty come into early childhood programs and primary schools with significantly different language backgrounds. Although these children often use language effectively within their families and homes, they face problems in schools where the vocabulary and language structure is more like that of an economically favored child.

Children living in poverty are also more likely to have a parent with a low level of education. Educational level is linked with how parents talk to, play with, and read to young children (Bradley et al., 1989). Children living in poverty also are more likely to be homeless and live in neighborhoods where violence occurs.

It is important to remember, however, that despite these statistics and concerns, educators should not assume that a child from an economically disadvantaged environment is automatically going to have difficulty in school. "At risk" means a likely area of concern but not causation. Many children come from homes that are economically disadvantaged and do not have difficulty learning to read (Snow et al., 1998). In the same way, many parents who live in poverty, against great odds and through strong commitment, provide a positive learning environment and secure base for their children.

PRACTICAL STRATEGIES
Judy Harris Helm and Jean Lang

Throughout our years of working with children, we have seen the doors to the world of school open for many poor children during the process of doing a project. One of the greatest advantages of project work for children in poverty is the motivation for learning academic skills and the opportunity for meaningful practice and perfection of these skills. As they eagerly search through books to find answers to questions, label their drawings, make literacy materials for play environments, and struggle to write their questions and thoughts, they discover that literacy is a valuable tool. We have seen the same development with mathematical skills. Children learn that counting, measuring, and solving problems using math are useful skills to learn. Project work is the closest a child can come to the world of work, and it is often while doing a project that a child first sees the relevance of learning these skills to adult jobs. This is especially important for children who do not live in optimal environments.

Children's self-images change during project work. They begin to see themselves as learners and problem solvers; they build self-confidence in their ability to find answers to their own questions; and they learn that adults can be resources of information and assistance. These experiences increase their ability to cope and find solutions to problems within their home environments.

We have observed that projects become a vehicle for the development of strong relationships between teachers and families. A project can provide a common focus for parents, children, school personnel, and even members of the larger community. All of these people come together for the purpose of helping children in their investigations and supporting the growth of children's knowledge, skills, and dispositions toward learning. They also widen families' awareness of resources available in their communities.

Not all project work will automatically provide these benefits for children living in poverty. In our work with classrooms and teachers, we have realized eight practical strategies that teachers can use to maximize the effectiveness of project work for children living in poverty.

Practical Strategy 1: Maximize Opportunities for Self-Initiated Learning

Self-initiated learning occurs in project work as children choose and explore materials and artifacts, select activities, and create structures or play environments. Children can learn how to take independent action and solve problems with minimum adult help. Grotberg (1995) identifies these skills as building blocks of resiliency. By maximizing the opportunities for self-initiated learning that occur in project work, teachers are providing opportunities for children to develop the inner strengths of self-confidence and self-esteem.

One way teachers can maximize self-initiation is to consider children's interests when selecting the topic for a project. After a topic is chosen, teachers can also involve children in determining what they want to know about that topic and what they want to investigate within the project. For example, self-initiated learning occurred when the study of an author turned into a museum project. The teacher introduced children to books by Eric Carle and showed how his pictures were different from those in other books. They became interested in collages, so the teacher read books about art to the children, including a book that mentioned an art museum. Most of the children had never been to a museum and had many questions about the museum in the book. The teacher followed the children's interest and arranged a visit to an art museum. This project extended for some time and included the study of various art media, tours, tour guides, and galleries. They made a classroom museum with exhibits on sculpture, painting, collage, and drawing and conducted tours of their museum at the end of the project.

Teachers can maximize self-initiated learning in projects by allocating enough time for it to occur. The class that participated in the Airplane Project, described below, stayed focused on the topic for ten weeks even though there were two major interruptions in their school schedule. We have observed that children's attention spans during project-related activities are longer than during other classroom activities. Deep engagement in project work enables the development of more complex questions for investigation. Extended study encourages children to continue to think about the project away from school, discuss it with parents, and take independent action as they bring relevant materials into the classroom.

Maximizing self-initiation in project work does not require that topics emerge totally from the children. Teachers can initiate topics for study. In working with children who have had few experiences outside the home or beyond the block where they live, we have found it helpful to introduce children to a variety of topics. The teacher often initiates a topic and then observes children's interests as they develop background knowledge about it before a decision is made to proceed with a project (Helm & Katz, 2001; Katz & Chard, 1989). An example of this is the Sheep Project, which was initiated by the teacher. It was spring, and the children were discussing visits to a petting zoo at the mall with their parents. To the teacher it seemed like a very limited way to observe animals, so she arranged to have a lamb visit school. She talked to the farmer who loaned the baby animals to the petting zoo at the mall. He agreed to bring a lamb into the classroom for one day. The children were able to observe, touch, and sketch the lamb in the classroom setting. With that background, they were then able to think of many questions. It was the teacher's initiative in bringing the lamb to the class that enabled the children to develop the background knowledge necessary to then take control of the investigation.

Practical Strategy 2:
Support Children's Emotional Involvement in Learning

Teachers can help children develop resiliency by providing opportunities for them to identify their feelings and talk about them (Grotberg, 1995). During project work, teachers can maximize emotional involvement by encouraging and supporting discussions about how the children feel about what they are doing. We have observed many instances of children sharing their excitement about learning something new and talking about that excitement. In a classroom with second-language learners, the teacher told the children that arrangements had been made for them to visit a flower shop. The children responded positively but not with great enthusiasm until one of the children said, "You

mean this is a trip we get to ask questions and take our clipboards and draw stuff? Cool!" Immediately the children became excited and eager for the visit. This story illustrates the difference between the emotional involvement generated by typical classroom activities, such as a traditional field trip, compared with project activities, such as a field-site visit.

The documentation that occurs during project work also provides an opportunity for children to talk about the events and experiences of a project. Even very young children are able to see the differences between first, second, or third attempts at drawing, painting, or writing. They often express pride in their work or talk about working hard, being frustrated, or mastering a skill. As one child commented to a teacher after he had worked through a particularly challenging problem, "I must be a genius to have thought of that!" (Helm, Beneke, & Steinheimer, 1998, p. 102). Viewing documentation at culminating events such as open houses or project parties is an excellent way to celebrate the accomplishments of the project and to focus parent-child conversations on the developing knowledge, skills, and dispositions of the children.

Practical Strategy 3:
Focus on the Environment and Culture of the Child

In classrooms where children have had limited experiences outside the home, it is especially important to support topics of study that are based on the child's environment. Projects that focus on the child's neighborhood and immediate community are not only more likely to engage children's interest and lead to in-depth investigation, but they are also more likely to engage the interest and involvement of parents. Encouraging parental involvement is especially beneficial to children living in poverty. Projects can provide opportunities for exploration of stores, businesses, and neighborhoods in children's immediate environments, or even their own school or center. When a project relates to children's surroundings, they usually have some familiarity with the topic and can more easily express curiosity and develop their own questions. Again, the teacher does not have to wait for children's interest in these local sites to emerge. We have found that children who have not had many opportunities for self-initiated learning are unlikely to spontaneously generate questions and show intense curiosity. Interest and curiosity emerges, however, if the teacher provides an introduction to the topic. A teacher will often survey the neighborhood around a school by taking a walk with the children. She can expand the children's knowledge about places and things she thinks the children might find interesting but have had few opportunities to explore. It is helpful to document signs of interest or comments that the children make during this walk. They may become interested in a local construction site, the donut shop on the corner, or a passing fire truck. If the children express interest, a project may develop. If not, at least the teacher has introduced them to new components of their community and broadened their knowledge.

Introducing children to topics of study within their own neighborhood or the area around their school or center also makes it more likely that the experience will be culturally relevant to children and families. A neighborhood store where the families shop is more likely to have foods that are part of the child's life and literacy materials, such as labels and signs in the language used by the children's families. A local restaurant might be where the children eat or a parent works. A bus stop or a subway station may be an important place in the life of the family.

Topics that grow from explorations of the community and neighborhood are often easily related to curriculum goals. For example, a project about a local fire station is likely to involve learning about how people help each other through their jobs—a common social studies goal. Projects about neighborhood birds, animals, or the weather are related to science curriculum goals. Focusing projects on these topics will help build background knowledge for study in elementary school. In homes with more economic resources than in less affluent families, these issues are often topics of ongoing conversations between parents and children.

Practical Strategy 4:
Encourage the Strengthening of Intellectual Dispositions

It is important that children growing up in poverty develop dispositions to use academic skills, to read and write, and to think reflectively. When guiding projects with children, it is important to provide ample opportunities for children to

• Make sense of their experience
• Theorize, analyze, hypothesize, and synthesize
• Make and check predictions
• Find information on their own
• Strive for accuracy
• Be empirical
• Grasp the consequences of actions
• Persist in seeking solutions to problems
• Speculate about cause-effect relationships
• Predict others' wishes and feelings (Helm & Katz, 2001)

Children in middle- and upper-income families are often encouraged to discuss their ideas, answer questions, and explain their thinking. For example, one of the questions that the children had during the Airplane Project was "What button makes the plane go up?" This created much discussion. When thinking about the "up button" on the airplane, the children developed their own hypotheses and then were able to determine the accuracy of their ideas during the field-site visit to the airport. During the Sheep Project, one of the questions was "How do you get the wool off?" The children offered possible solutions. One child thought they used a knife or a saw. "No, they use scissors," answered another. During the field-site visit, the children asked Frank, who sheared the sheep, what he used to get the wool off the sheep, and he showed them his electric shears.

The children offered other hypotheses during the Sheep Project, including about what sheep eat:

"They eat dirt."
"No, they don't eat dirt."
"They eat grass."

During the site visit, the children tested their hypothesis and observed that sheep eat hay, milk, and corn. They also thought about where sheep come from:

"Do they come from eggs?"
"No!"

The children found the answer to their question when they had the opportunity to feel the baby lambs moving inside the mother ewes.

Practical Strategy 5:
Encourage Children to Solve Their Own Problems and Practice Social Skills

Children have many opportunities in project work to learn to work with others. Research suggests that there is a relationship between the roles that children have in determining their own learning experiences and the development of social skills. A study of kindergarten classes using three different teaching approaches (direct instruction, a constructivist approach based on child-initiated activities, and an eclectic approach) found that the children from the constructivist class were more interpersonally interactive. They exhibited a greater number and variety of negotiation strategies and shared more experiences (DeVries, Reese-Learned, & Morgan, 1991). When learners take responsibility for their work, are self-regulated, and are able to define their goals and evaluate their accomplishments, they are energized by their work; their dispositions to solve problems, to seek deeper understanding, can be developed and strengthened (Jones et al., 1994).

Teachers can also engender social development as children learn to share the work of the project. Children are encouraged to sign up for various jobs based on their interests and questions, and they work in teams and learn to rely on others to get information they need. For example, during the field-site visit to the airport during the Airplane Project, the children signed up to sketch one part of the airplane. The same subdivision of labor was used in constructing the airplane, and the children used their sketches as a plan for construction. The youngest children assisted with the painting of the plane. Lexie, Nick, and Adrianna wanted to work on attaching the back of the plane to the cockpit. Adam, Olivia, and Joey decided to construct the wings. Raymond, Brittany, and David wanted to work on the door and window. The children offered suggestions for the construction process. "Poke a few holes for windows," offered Olivia. "We could cut the wings out with scissors," David suggested. "We could paint it or color it," said Rachel and Joey. The afternoon class chose to focus on the interior of the plane. They put rows of chairs inside the plane and numbered them. Mikey, Caleb, Nick, and Zachary played inside the airplane; they used a doll high chair for the "potty." All of these children made a contribution to the project as a whole.

Project work also provides a context for leadership skills to emerge. Teachers can increase the value of project work by standing back and giving children opportunities to develop leadership skills. The more experienced children tend to lead discussions, formulate questions, and serve as models to the younger, less experienced children, who then learn by observing the student leaders. The following year these younger children become the leaders of the group. Children also mentor each other. We have observed that children appear to attend more to the theories and conclusions of their peers than to adults who simply tell them the right answer.

One of the biggest challenges and benefits for children in project work is to learn how to work together to solve problems. Using communication and problem-solving skills to resolve interpersonal problems or knowing how and when to seek help from adults are resiliency skills that extend beyond the classroom. Encouraging the children to work out their own problems and disagreements while participating in project work is important. In the Airplane Project, Joey, Adam, and Wesley tried to use a small box that the children thought could be used as the cockpit. They realized that the box was too small and as a group decided it would be necessary to use a larger box. Sometimes disagreements can help the children revise their plans. These changes require compromise, negotiation, and conflict resolution.

Practical Strategy 6: Maximize Opportunities for Parent Involvement

Parents become very interested and involved in projects, and the project becomes something that children and parents talk about at home. Parents serve as visiting experts and answer children's questions; assist in the teaching of relevant skills, such as how to assemble something out of wood; and become colearners as they explore the topic alongside their children. Project work also provides opportunities for parents to observe teachers interacting with children. For example, a parent accompanying a class on a field-site visit may see how the teacher draws the children's attention to an object or process. A parent's expectations for his or her own children may rise. We have observed that parents are often surprised at how well their young children can draw, write, count, and photograph.

Practical Strategy 7: Emphasize the Role of Literacy

Learning to read can be challenging for many children living in poverty; there is a relationship between income level and language development (Smith, Brooks-Gunn, & Klebanov, 1997). Development of a good vocabulary in the early years is important for emerging literacy. Children can learn many words about the project topic and use these words in role-play and conversations. New vocabulary can be introduced during project work and definitions of familiar words refined. For example, at the beginning of the Sheep Project, children referred to the wool as "fur." By the end of the project, they had a clear understanding of the word *wool* and many other words related to the project. When project topics relate to the standard curriculum, children develop a familiarity with words they will read and study in elementary school. For example, in a project on spring gardens, children learned about bulbs and seeds and the planting process.

Teachers can use projects to strengthen young children's motivation to master a wide variety of academic skills, especially reading and writing. In a study of first-grade children doing both projects and formal units, children were more involved in reading and research in the project then in the teacher-directed unit (Bryson, 1994). For example, children are often observed attempting to read signs, pamphlets, and books to find answers to the questions generated in Phase I of the project. During the Airplane Project, teachers read and

Figure 3.1 Children refer to sketches and field notes for construction.

discussed books about airplanes and travel. They brought in many books, charts, and magazines that helped the children extend their knowledge of airplanes. The children learned that books, magazines, and the Internet can be used as resources to increase their knowledge. As young investigators create play environments, block structures, buildings, and other products related to the project, they can be encouraged to identify the parts of their structure. For example, children involved in the Mexican Restaurant Project made money, menus, signs, and coupons for their restaurant (see Chapter 6).

Many opportunities for writing occur naturally in project work. Children write to record what they are observing on field-site visits or to communicate with experts. Play environments created during project work result in many literacy products. In the Airplane Project, adults modeled the writing process while taking dictation from the children for lists of materials and parts of the airplane. Children copied identification numbers and letters on the airplane at the field-site visit. They referred back to these sketches, field notes, and photos when constructing their plane (see Figure 3.1). More specific strategies for moving children toward literacy are discussed in chapter 4.

Practical Strategy 8: Maintain High Expectations and Standards

It is important for the teacher to maintain high standards and expectations of children. Throughout the project, teachers have many opportunities to select materials, ask questions, and provoke thought. Although it is important to remain developmentally appropriate, teachers need to guard against narrowing experiences for children who come to school with limited backgrounds. All children need to be encouraged equally to think creatively, clarify their thoughts, and stretch their minds.

CONCLUSION

Careful facilitation of project work supports the development of knowledge, skills, and dispositions to achieve in school and provides opportunities for children to develop positive self-esteem and resiliency. As discussed above, the following practical strategies will maximize the benefits of project work for children living in poverty:

1. Maximize opportunities for self-initiated learning
2. Support children's emotional involvement in learning
3. Focus on the environment and culture of the child
4. Encourage the strengthening of intellectual dispositions
5. Encourage children to solve their own problems and practice social skills
6. Maximize opportunities for parent involvement
7. Emphasize the role of literacy
8. Maintain high expectations and standards

The next part of this chapter shows how these strategies can be enacted in project work through the description of an actual project. Throughout the story of the project, specific strategies are highlighted by number and short phrases shown in italics.

THE AIRPLANE PROJECT
Jean Lang

The Airplane Project took place at the Fairview Early Childhood Center in Rockford, Illinois. Rockford is an urban school district serving approximately 1,600 three- to five-year-olds. The children come from diverse backgrounds: 27% are African American, 25% Hispanic, and 5% Asian. Almost 70% of the students are from low-income families. Children are selected for the program based on cognitive, language, and motor skills that qualify them as at risk for school failure. Environmental risk factors are also considered in determining eligibility. The Airplane Project began in mid-March and culminated in May of 2001, lasting a total of ten weeks. Associate teacher Deb Frieman and student teacher Bob McCulloh collaborated with me on this project.

I teach two groups of children, one in the morning and one in the afternoon, with 18 students enrolled in each class, which means I work with 36 children and their families. Our program is completely integrated—we serve children with a variety of special needs in a shared setting. Each of my classes includes children with special needs, speech and language needs, and cultural and environmental risk factors.

One of my biggest challenges is finding a way to encourage parents from lower economic backgrounds to get involved in school activities. We believe that in order to provide an optimum learning environment, it is essential that families and staff be mutually supportive. When this relationship is in place, the children are nurtured. My colleagues and I work to communicate our belief that teachers and families alike can contribute to the children and the school. We believe that all families have resources and strengths to share. The involvement and support of parents is apparent in the documentation of the Airplane Project.

PHASE I: BEGINNING THE PROJECT

The children's interest in airplanes emerged in mid-March. There were both benefits and problems with the timing of this interest. The project benefited from the solid relationships with the children's families I was able to build during the previous months of the school. The class was right in the middle of preparation for our spring program, however, and spring break was not far behind. I wondered if the children's interest in the topic would remain strong in spite of these interruptions.

I realized that airplanes was a possible topic for a new project when the children began to notice and ask questions about the contrails left by jet airplanes that flew overhead (PS1: *Maximize self-initiated learning*). About this time the children spontaneously began to make paper airplanes and asked for my help. I soon had paper airplanes zooming all over my classroom. I could have said, "Put those away, we don't fly airplanes inside the classroom," but I did not. Frankly, I was tempted, but I recognized the potential of this activity to benefit my children, especially those who were living in poverty, in several important ways. For example, the study of the paper airplanes was child-initiated. It was also an activity that many of them had engaged in at home—it was part of their culture (PS3: *Focus on child's culture*). As they experimented with their designs, I could see the potential of the topic to challenge the children intellectually. It was also obvious that the children were emotionally involved in and engaged with the thrill of designing, making, and flying the paper airplanes (PS2: *Support emotional involvement*). I suspected that many of the children's parents might be able to assist their children with the investigation. So, instead of ending the paper airplane throwing, I encouraged the children to organize it (PS5: *Encourage problem solving and social skills*). For example, within the classroom, I challenged them to fly their airplanes so that they would land in a box on the other side of the room. The children were also allowed to fly their airplanes in the hallway so that they could see whose would fly the farthest.

Next, I made a teacher anticipatory planning web to determine if the children's interest in airplanes could become a project that would meet both standards and program goals (see Figure 3.2). Our program employs the Illinois Early Learning Standards and uses the Work Sampling Assessment System. Bob, Deb, and I brainstormed all the possible concepts or pieces of information about airplanes that might be of interest to the children. We also added to the web the potential portfolio items that might be collected in a project on airplanes.

After creating the anticipatory web, we felt confident that a project on airplanes had great potential to meet our goals and standards. As we looked over the concepts and information on the web, we predicted that the children would be interested in exploring the different kinds of airplanes. However, I have worked with children long enough to know that they are full of surprises. I recognized that they might just as easily become interested in the conveyor belt used to move the luggage into the airplane!

We began to bring in materials and do activities that would expand the children's interest in airplanes. For example, we folded airplanes with the children, brought

Figure 3.2 Concepts, subconcepts, curriculum goals, and potential portfolio items were webbed to explore the potential of airplanes as a project topic.

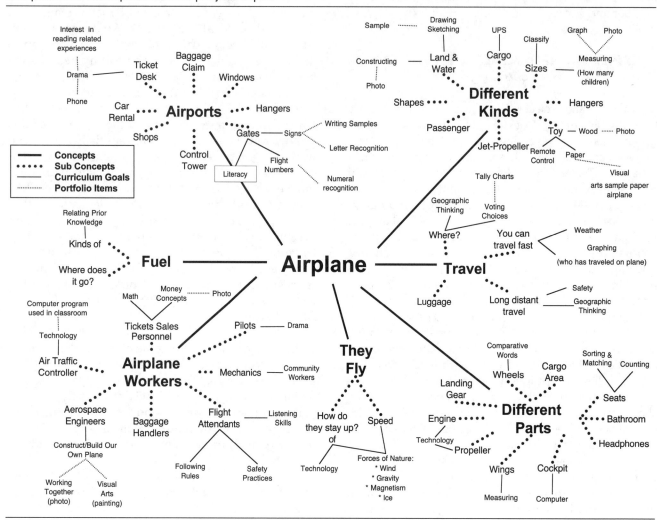

in books with pictures of airplanes, and read many books about airplanes (PS7: *Emphasize literacy*). We put up a poster in the classroom with all kinds of vehicles for air transportation, including hot air balloons, blimps, early airplane models, helicopters, and other modern aircraft (see Figure 3.3). We also brought in several model airplanes for the block area.

Children sketched their favorite airplanes during Phase I. We had used sketching as a learning activity for some time. We encouraged the children to focus on the shapes they observed in the object they are sketching and emphasize this as an observation activity, not an art activity. It was interesting to see that the children who had been with us earlier in the school year naturally mentored the children who were newer to the program and unfamiliar with our sketching process (PS5: *Encourage problem solving and social skills*; PS8: *Maintain high expectations and standards*).

As the children's interest intensified, we started to web with them to determine their current level of knowledge about airplanes (see Figure 3.4) and gather their questions (PS4: *Strengthen intellectual dispositions*).

The questions were not collected all at once but instead were gathered over time. They revealed the children's previous experiences with airplanes and the project approach.

1. Why do people buckle their seats?
2. What are the numbers on the plane for?
3. Is there a wheel that comes out right at the front?
4. Are there lights on the plane?
5. Can you sit anywhere you want?
6. Are there planes that go farther than Mexico? Will it crash if it does?
7. What button makes it go up?
8. How do they get to the cargo area?

Figure 3.3 In Phase I of the project, children were interested in a poster showing many types of aircraft.

9. What does that guy on the runway with the lights do?
10. What is that thing called that comes out of the plane when it lands?
11. What happens if the battery goes out?
12. Are there windows on the plane?

The second-year students served as models and mentors for the newer students. Their questions revealed a wide range of knowledge and past experience. For example, Mikey asked, "Are there planes that go farther than Mexico? Will it crash if it does?" This question revealed that Mikey had visited relatives in Mexico. Three-year-old Madison's simple question, "Are there windows on the plane," reflected her lack of experience with airplanes and question making (PS3: *Focus on child's culture*).

Deb, Bob, and I made a list of the children's questions and later made question cards (see Figure 3.5). The cards were illustrated and each was labeled with the name of the child who had asked the question. This

Figure 3.4 The children's initial knowledge about airplanes was gathered in a web.

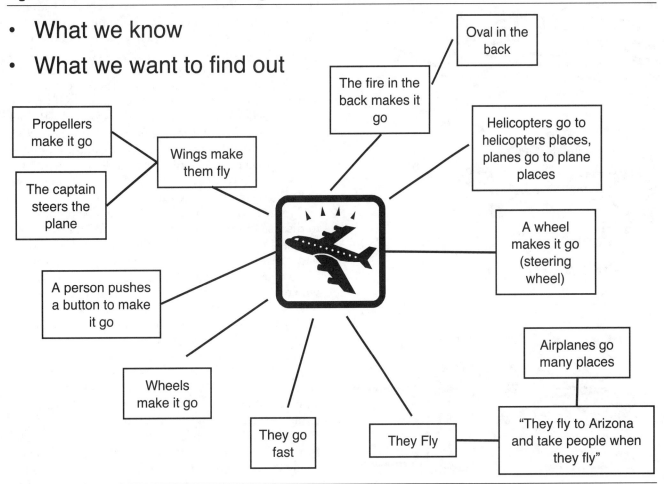

- # What we know
- # What we want to find out

Oval in the back

The fire in the back makes it go

Helicopters go to helicopters places, planes go to plane places

Propellers make it go

Wings make them fly

The captain steers the plane

A wheel makes it go (steering wheel)

A person pushes a button to make it go

Wheels make it go

They go fast

They Fly

Airplanes go many places

"They fly to Arizona and take people when they fly"

allowed the children to see the parent volunteers record the answers on the back of the cards (PS7: *Emphasize the role of literacy*), which was one way we planned to involve parents from diverse backgrounds (PS6: *Maximize parent involvement*).

PHASE II: INVESTIGATION

We prepared for our field-site visit by making travel arrangements, finding parent volunteers, and making calls to Emery Air Charter (PS6: *Maximize parent involvement*). Emery manages all the charter and private

Figure 3.5 Question cards showing the children's questions about airplanes.

planes, as well as the military planes, at the Rockford airport. This small, local airport was just the right size for our children. Our staff made a pre–site visit to the airport to look around, and we discussed the children's questions with Matt, the airport supervisor who would be our field guide. When I called Matt to schedule our pre–site visit, I told him that we would be bringing a list of the children's questions, and he chuckled. When we showed him the children's questions, however, he was quite impressed.

We also discussed the schedule of the children's visit with Matt. We knew that we wanted to spend the bulk of our time at the airplane hangar, but we wanted to be sure we would have enough time for the children to see the entire airport, including the baggage claim and ticket counter. Matt helped us develop an alternate plan in case of inclement weather so that the children could still sketch and get inside a real airplane. We also talked with Matt about possible artifacts and materials that the airport might donate to our classroom to use in dramatic play and construction. The pre–site visit was vitally important to the success of our field-site visit. Matt learned that our children were serious students who had real questions they wanted answered. He began to see the children as investigators and learners.

We were a little nervous about the fact that the morning group only had three questions, and we wondered if they would have a successful site visit. On the day of the trip, however, when the children were right there in front of real airplanes that they could reach out and touch, they spontaneously came up with many more questions. For example, three-year-old Rachel looked at the fresh-air intake on the plane and asked, "What is that little hole?" I learned about the air intake and many other aspects of airplanes along with my students. I was impressed with the children's knowledge and interest, and so was Matt!

We met with the parent volunteers before the trip to discuss the purpose and process of field sketching and asking questions. We explained that the children had signed up to sketch particular parts of the airplane, but we also wanted to encourage them to sketch the whole plane. We held a discussion with parents about how much support they should give to the children as they investigated airplanes and the airport (see Figure 3.6; PS6: *Maximize parent involvement*).

On the day of the field trip, two children were assigned to each parent, who carried a bag with a clipboard and a set of question cards. Three families videotaped the trip and later shared copies with us. I was reminded that it is important not to make assumptions about a family's resources, skills, or strengths when the first parent to volunteer to videotape the trip was a person with very limited financial resources. I mistakenly assumed that he did not have access to a video camera,

Figure 3.6 Parents were coached ahead of time in how to support field-site sketching.

and I would have to provide one for him. This caution about assumptions is especially important for teachers who work in schools where there are many children living in poverty (PS6: *Maximize parent involvement*).

Parents also took, and later shared, photographs of the field trip. They helped the children with their sketching by giving verbal encouragement and asking the children to look for basic shapes and details (see Figure 3.7; PS4: *Strengthen intellectual dispositions*). Two boxes on the bottom of the sketching paper were used to indicate whether the work was done with or without adult help.

In the days following the field-site visit, we revisited the airport through the videos filmed by volunteer parents. These videos were a great contribution to the growth of our project. The children used them to continue to make sketches of what was seen on the trip (see Figures 3.8 & 3.9) and to add to our web (PS4: *Encourage intellectual dispositions*).

As the children thought more about airplanes, we hoped that one of them would come up with the idea of making an airplane. Sure enough, Joey said, "I got an idea. We could make our own airplane out of cardboard" (PS1: *Maximize self-initiated learning*). We soon began to gather objects and materials that could be used in the construction of the class airplane.

Parents became very involved with this aspect of the project. A parent who delivered appliances saved boxes for us to use in the construction. Parents also volunteered to help with the actual classroom

Figure 3.7 Field sketch of Lockheed Vegas.

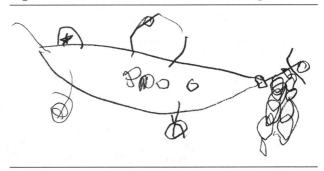

Figure 3.8 Four-year-old Adam used the videotape as a reference for his Time 2 sketch of Lockheed Vegas.

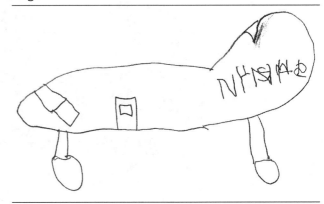

Figure 3.9 Sketch of communication radio by five-year-old Olivia.

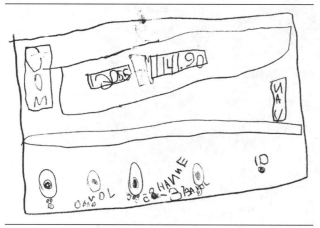

construction of the plane. We kept them informed of our progress through our weekly newsletter, which included photos and stories about our frustrations and successes. It seemed that parents were just as excited about the construction of the airplane as the children! (PS6: *Maximize parent involvement*). We actually built two airplanes—the children decided that our first airplane was too small (see Figure 3.10), so we began to construct a bigger model.

One of the frustrations both the children and teachers experienced involved how to support the cardboard wings. They were too thin and kept drooping down.

Mikey came up with the idea of using a brace to support the floppy wings. He looked at the pictures from the field-site visit and said, "We need to make a cut like this" (PS4: *Encourage intellectual dispositions*). As he talked, he used his hands to indicate a diagonal cut. He also said, "My dad has a saw, and he could help." The next day Mikey's father, Martin, came to help the children fix the droopy wings. Mikey's father spoke very little English, but he was still able to be a resource to the children for their project (see Figure 3.11; PS6: *Maximize parent involvement*).

We also had trouble getting the steering wheel to move up and down and turn from side to side. It kept coming off of the control panel. One night I received a call at home from a family who had been discussing the problem. They thought they had a solution and wanted to come in the next day to try it out. Nate's mom, Susan, brought her own drill and some PVC pipe to our classroom and helped the children fix the steering wheel (see Figure 3.12). Nate's father also donated several switches and gauges from the company where he worked, which manufactured aircraft parts (PS6: *Maximize parent involvement*).

One of the biggest challenges we faced in the construction of the airplane was cutting the cardboard and constructing the cockpit that contained the heavy gauges and instruments the children brought back from the field-site visit. The children traced around the instruments, and the teachers used heavy weight glue to attach them to the cockpit. The teachers also helped

Figure 3.10 The first airplane the children constructed was too small for their dramatic play.

Figure 3.11 Mikey's dad solves the problem of the droopy wings.

Figure 3.12 Nate's mom uses her drill to make the steering wheel movable.

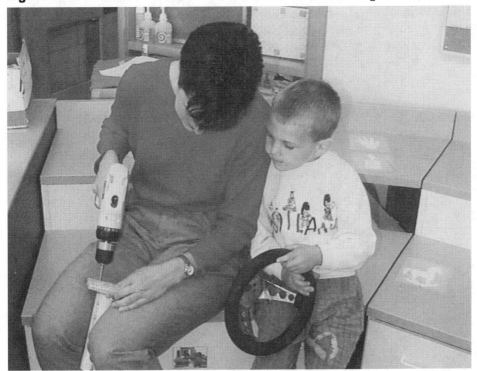

with cutting the cardboard. This was more assistance than we would have preferred to provide, but we try to balance safety and independence in project work.

Many opportunities to learn and apply new knowledge, skills, and dispositions developed during the Airplane Project (PS4: *Encourage intellectual dispositions*). Both the morning and the afternoon classes worked on the same airplane. This became an opportunity to use the skills and talents of children from both classes. The children learned to work together as a team, not only with their own class, but also with the class that attended the other half of the day (PS5: *Encourage problem solving and social skills*). For example, the children in both classes voted to decide the placement of the instruments in the cockpit and the type of airplane wings to construct. The two classes also voted to decide what color to paint the plane. The discussions about the votes were communicated between the classes through tally charts and notes. Even the youngest children were able to participate when it was time to apply the colored paint to the exterior (PS5: *Encourage problem solving and social skills*).

Tickets and seating presented another opportunity to stretch children's thinking. The children numbered the chairs that represented the seats of the plane. We discussed tickets and how they could indicate which seat a passenger must sit in on the plane (PS4: *Encourage intellectual dispositions*).

The Airplane Project provided many opportunities for dramatic play and sparked imaginations (see Figure 3.13). For example, the children shared their wishes about where they wanted to go in the airplane. One

child wanted to fly to Oklahoma to see his mother and brother (PS2: *Support emotional involvement*).

PHASE III: CONCLUDING THE PROJECT

With only a few days of school left, Susan Stethens, a reporter from WNIJ public radio station, came to interview the children about their project. Susan was working on a project called *FLYKIDS*, which focused on young people's interest in flying planes, so she asked if she could interview some of our students. The children's intellectual dispositions and attitudes about themselves as learners had been influenced positively by this project. For example, when interviewed, Joey said to Susan, "When I grow up, I wanna' be . . . I wanna' be . . . I wanna' be a pilot." Joey's view of himself and his future had been changed. He saw himself in the seat of an airplane flying high in the sky, and he knew he could control his own future (PS4: *Strengthen intellectual dispositions*).

TEACHER REFLECTIONS

It takes a lot of courage to keep an airplane the size of a refrigerator box in your classroom for eight weeks (see Figure 3.14), but it was sad when we had to dismantle it. I am thankful that we have a record of it in our documentation of the children's work.

Using the project approach with children from all SES backgrounds is beneficial, but I believe it is espe-

Figure 3.13 Two girls are seated in the cockpit and pretend to pilot the finished airplane.

Figure 3.14 The finished airplane, complete with cockpit, wheels, and passenger windows.

cially helpful for children living in poverty. Project work allows children to construct their own learning and create their own goals and areas of investigation. It provides meaningful ways for parents to become involved in their children's education, and, most important, project work allows children to view themselves as successful learners and to believe that they will be successful learners in the future.

REFERENCES

Beneke, S. (1998). *Rearview mirror: Reflections on a preschool car project.* Champaign, IL: ERIC Clearinghouse on Elementary and Early Childhood Education.

Bradley, M. H., Caldwell, B. M., Rock, S. L., Ramey, C. T., Barnard, K. E., Gray, C., Hammond, M. A., Mitchell, S., Gottfried, A. W., Siegel, L., & Johnson, D. L. (1989). Home environment and cognitive development in the first three years of life: A collaborative study involving six sites and three ethnic groups in North America. *Developmental Psychology, 25,* 217–35.

Bryson, E. (1994). *Will a project approach to learning provide children opportunities to do purposeful reading and writing, as well as provide opportunities for authentic learning in other curriculum areas?* Urbana, IL: ERIC Clearinghouse on Elementary and Early Childhood Education.

Child poverty fact sheet. (2001, June). New York: National Center for Children in Poverty, Columbia University.

DeVries, R., Reese-Learned, H., & Morgan, P. (1991). Sociomoral development in direct-instruction, eclectic and constructivist kindergartens: A study of children's enacted interpersonal understandings. *Early Childhood Research & Practice, 6*(4), 473–517.

Duncan, G. J., & Brooks-Gunn, J. (Eds.). (1997). *Consequences of growing up poor.* New York: Russell Sage Foundation.

Grotberg, E. H. (1995). *A guide to promoting resilience in children: Strengthening the human spirit.* The Hague, The Netherlands: Bernard Van Leer Foundation.

Hart, B., & Risley, T. R. (1995). *Meaningful differences in the everyday experience of young American children.* Baltimore, MD: Paul H. Brooks Publishing Company.

Helm, J. H., Beneke, S., & Steinheimer, K. (1998). *Windows on learning: Documenting young children's work.* New York: Teachers College Press.

Helm, J. H., & Katz, L. G. (2001). *Young investigators: The project approach in the early years.* New York: Teachers College Press.

Jones, B., Valdez, G., Norakowski, J., & Rasmussen, C. (1994). *Designing learning and technology for educational reform.* Oak Brook, IL: North Central Regional Educational Laboratory.

Katz, L. G., & Chard, S. C. (1989). *Engaging children's minds: The project approach.* Greenwich, CT: Ablex Publishing Corporation.

Smith, J. R., Brooks-Gunn, J., & Klebanov, P. K. (1997). Consequences of living in poverty for young children's cognitive and verbal ability and early school achievement. In G. J. Duncan & Jeanne Brooks-Gunn (Eds.), *Consequences of growing up poor* (pp. 132–89). New York: Russell Sage Foundation.

Snow, C. E., Burns, M. S., & Griffin, P. (Eds.). (1998). *Preventing reading difficulties in young children.* Washington, DC: National Academy Press.

CHAPTER 4

Moving Young Children Toward Literacy

Contributors: Judy Harris Helm, Mary Ann Gottlieb, and Jean O'Mara-Thieman

DEFINING THE CHALLENGE
Judy Harris Helm

A variety of skills are needed for successful reading. According to the National Research Council, when children begin to learn to read they need instruction that focuses on using reading to obtain meaning from print, awareness of sounds and groups of letters, and an understanding of the writing system, particularly letters and sequences of letters in words. They also need frequent opportunities to read and write. To make adequate progress in reading and writing, children must develop a working understanding of how sounds are represented alphabetically and frequently use reading for meaning so that they can monitor their understanding and repair misunderstandings (Snow, Burns, & Griffin, 1998). The challenge to teachers is to move young children toward the literacy goal by ensuring that each and every child receives these experiences and instruction, yet do it in such a way that interest and motivation to master the skill is preserved.

Another challenge of literacy instruction comes from the integral relationship between reading and culture: there is clearly a cultural component to the process of learning to read. According to Jerome Bruner (1996), learning and thinking are always *situated* in a cultural setting and dependent upon the utilization of cultural resources. It is important to teach literacy in such a way that it affirms the cultural identities of students of diverse backgrounds:

An expanded definition of literacy goes beyond skills to include people's willingness to use literacy, the con-nections between reading and writing, the dynamic process of constructing meaning (including the role of cultural schemata), and the importance of printed text. Social context is a particularly important concept for teachers to consider, both in terms of understanding literacy and of understanding how typical school literacy lessons might need to be adjusted to be more beneficial for students of diverse backgrounds. (Au, 1993, p. 33)

Children who are learning a second language or children who differ from the mainstream in ethnicity or social class have added challenges in learning literacy skills when these skills are defined only by American mainstream culture. This is especially true if educators are not sensitive to the diversity of cultures of the children in their classrooms and how literacy experiences are meaningful to them.

Parents also have cultural expectations for how their children will learn to read, which may or may not be similar to the teacher's expectations. For example, a parent may think that young children need to spend extensive time copying letter shapes. If the teacher is able to combine research about children learning to read with culturally responsive teaching practices that respect and incorporate the expectations of the family, then the child benefits. As a result, the teacher is more likely to promote social and cultural inclusion, improve academic achievement, and empower parents as advocates for their child's education (Meier, 2000). Part of the challenge of moving young children toward literacy is to listen carefully, incorporate the child's culture into the reading process, and integrate literacy into meaningful learning experiences.

PRACTICAL STRATEGIES
Mary Ann Gottlieb

While I was teaching at the Valeska Hinton Early Childhood Education Center, helping children become literate was one of my major challenges as well as one of my primary goals. Valeska Hinton is an urban public school in Peoria, Illinois, for at-risk 3-, 4-, 5-, and 6-year-old children. Most of my classes were multi-age, 4/5 or 5/6, and looped for two years.

I have found that the project approach offers many opportunities for literacy development through reading, writing, speaking, and listening. Each of these aspects of literacy is crucial to the development of young children, and as a teacher, I believe that we must provide experiences within which literacy in all its forms can develop. The project approach supports the strategies that lead to mastery of these components.

READING

Practical Strategy 1:
Emphasize Building Vocabulary as a Foundation for Further Learning

According to Adams (1990), children must have considerable exposure to numerous interesting reading materials to encourage vocabulary development. Varied and profuse literacy experiences, along with phonics instruction, are needed to develop good readers. Early in a project, it is important to develop the vocabulary necessary to support the initial investigation. When beginning to explore a topic with young children, I plan experiences that expose them to vocabulary that is related to the emerging topic. "Learning is maximized when teachers lay the groundwork beforehand" (Neuman, Copple, & Bredekamp, 2000, p. 59). When I began the Farm Project, for example, reading informational books to the children about farms helped them become familiar with words about farm animals, farm machinery, and crops. Visiting a site early in the project also builds the background upon which further learning is built and reveals inaccuracies in understandings. For example, as we traveled to visit a dairy farm, one at-risk kindergartner called out, "Look at those black elephants." This child's concepts of cows and elephants prior to that trip were inaccurate. Taking the field trip at the beginning of the Farm Project helped develop vocabulary intrinsic to the project.

Sometimes photographs from the field experience are used to create vocabulary books. During the Farm Project, I asked each child to select two photos with which he or she was familiar. Then each child sat with me at the computer as I recorded his or her words. The pictures and accompanying dictated text helped to support the newly learned vocabulary related to the field experience (see Figure 4.1).

When the children listened to me read what they had said, I modeled the proofreading process. Together we corrected any errors, and then they typed their own names at the bottom of their paragraph, thereby taking ownership of it. The words were their words, and the writing now belonged to them. When young children see their words in print, they begin to realize that what they say can be written and read at a later time. The act of recording their words helps young children see the connection between speaking, writing, and reading. These kinds of demonstrations are an effective way to teach children critical concepts, such as developing word awareness (Neuman et al., 2000). Books documenting field experiences and new vocabulary become references for the rest of the project.

The field-experience books also can be shared with parents by sending them home on a rotating basis. Taking the book home gives every child the opportunity to share the project with his or her parents and practice using the new vocabulary. Parents can then encourage their child to use these words in conversation. Sending home the field-experience books becomes an opportunity to put meaningful books into the hands of families who may have limited access to appropriate reading materials in their homes.

The webbing process that takes place during project work is also an excellent way to build vocabulary. At the beginning of each project, we create a web (see Helm & Katz, 2001), which allows us to organize and classify the information the children currently know about a topic. The initial web is often incomplete or inaccurate; however, from this web, we help the children generate questions about the topic that will provide the direction for further investigation. Continual references to the web help expose the children to vocabulary about the topic. By the end of the project, some of the children may be able to recognize or write some of those words.

We make a final web at the end of each project, which is much more detailed and accurate than our initial web. In the Bakery Project, for example, the final web contained extensive information about the bakery itself, bakery products, baking experiences, and our own bakery sale. New vocabulary, unique to each project, often appears in the final web. When the beginning and final webs are placed side by side, the children are able to compare them and see the amount of information they have learned. Venn diagrams using the project vocabulary taken from the beginning and final webs are another way of observing vocabulary growth.

Figure 4.1 After choosing a picture taken during the farm field experience, Briana dictated commentary to the teacher, who typed it on the computer. Briana then typed her own name.

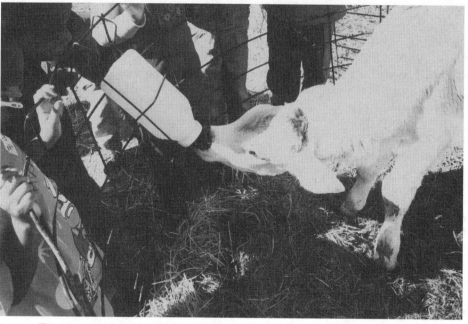

This is a little cow. He is drinking milk from a bottle. The farmer's wife brought that bottle for the baby calf. The calf gets milk two times every day.

Briana Ross

Practical Strategy 2:
Encourage Children to Play Around with Letter and Word Recognition

Snow, Burns, and Griffin (1998) point out that good phonological awareness in young children is a strong predictor of reading success. They must develop a basic awareness of the phonemic structure of language before they are able to identify beginning sounds in words. "Playing around" with project words presents children with many opportunities to use rhyme and alliteration, thus strengthening phonological awareness. Similarly, the joint statement of the International Reading Association and NAEYC states that "children learn about the sounds of language through exposure to *linguistic awareness* games, nursery rhymes, and rhythmic activities" (Neuman et al., 2000, p. 8).

Mastery of letter recognition and sounds is an exit goal for kindergartners in our school district. As part of Phase III of the Health Center project, the kindergartners created an alphabet of project-related words using the letters and sounds they had learned. Sometimes they were unable to recall facts or items beginning with a specific letter. If after several days we still could not recall words beginning with specific sounds, then we left that space blank.

A ambulance	D doctor	G
B Band-Aids	E emergency	H hospital
C cast	F fracture	I itch

This task was more difficult during the Mail Project, so my class of four- and five-year-olds sent the list to neighboring first graders who also participated in the project. They helped us recall mail-related words for some of the unused letters. Some of the project words expanded students' vocabularies, while others could be referenced for writing later in the year.

Practical Strategy 3:
Provide Opportunities for Publishing and Reading Child-Made Books

There are many opportunities to make books during a project. While at the field site, we usually sketch significant objects (see Figure 4.2). For example, during the Farm Project, we made repeated sketches of farm animals, referring to the photographs and video taken at the farm and our reference books. A group of children selected specific sketches and made individual farm books for each member of the class. These little books became part of our class-made book collection and were used during our daily "quiet reading time."

An accessible classroom library that provides "immediate access to books" encourages children to practice newly learned reading skills (Neuman et al., 2000). Each day we spend some time reading books. At the beginning of the year, the children look quietly at six or eight small books (picture books or easy readers) kept in individual plastic book boxes. The activity might last for two minutes. As the year progresses, the time is lengthened, and we add books that we have made during our small group times. Illustrated by each child, these three- or four-page books have repeated text. Every day we do this "quiet reading" after lunch (see Figure 4.3), although many of the children read aloud in a quiet voice, often inventing text. When the book boxes become crowded, some books are sent home to help build home libraries. The commercial books are exchanged monthly, and more are added as the children become familiar with the stories.

WRITING

Practical Strategy 4:
Provide Events That Encourage Writing

Young children need a variety of writing materials so they can experiment with recording their ideas and words. If teachers and parents accept scribble writing and invented spelling as natural and valid, children will be comfortable with writing. Parents and teachers should encourage children as they learn to write letters (Burns, Griffin, & Snow, 1999). The early letters will later become parts of words and then sentences. Invented spelling helps develop understanding of phoneme identity, phoneme segmentation, and sound-spelling relationships (Snow et al., 1998).

In project work, many events encourage and compel children to write, thus making writing purposeful. As questions arise about a project, the children sometimes use their writing skills to correspond with other classrooms. An older child might write as the younger child assists with the ideas or beginning sounds of words. Since the younger child's writing skills are just emerging, the older child becomes a role model. During the Health Center Project, the children of another preschool classroom who were working on the same project answered our questions after their teacher, Judy Cagle, read our letter to them (see Figure 4.4).

Figure 4.2 Jonathon sketches lions while his friends continue to look at the animals.

Figure 4.3 Melvin reads from his "book box." Some of the books are child-made, while others are commercial books.

Sometimes two or three of the children would come to our room to respond orally to our questions. At other times, an adult would write with a child, supplying words or sounds. These shared writing times allowed the children in each classroom to take ownership of the work while an adult provided the necessary modeling and support.

Practical Strategy 5:
Help Children Develop
E-Mail Relationships

E-mail is a convenient way for young children to write, and it challenges them to communicate through writing and to actively think about print (Neuman et al., 2000). An e-mail relationship can be developed with experts or other classrooms. We e-mailed an early childhood class in Eureka, Illinois, as questions arose while we worked on the Farm Project. My class, in an urban school, had limited experiences with farms. Pam Scranton's class, a prekindergarten program in a small rural town, had different experiences. They were able to answer our questions about hatching chickens since they had an incubator in their classroom. The e-mail relationship deepened at the end of the Farm Project when my and Judy Cagle's classes invited Pam and Stacy Berg's rural prekindergarten/special education classes to visit our school and participate in some farm-related activities.

Practical Strategy 6:
Help Children Create Pamphlets
and Brochures

Upon completion of the Health Center Project, we discussed ways to share our investigation with the rest of the school and the community. Students wanted to tell visitors about the Health Center they had constructed in the center court of our building, but they were unfamiliar with the terms *open house* and *pamphlet*. With Judy Cagle's help, they created an invitation to an open house and a pamphlet to distribute to visitors. This experience helped them learn "that the power of writing is expressing one's own ideas in ways that can be understood by others" (Neuman et al., 2000, p. 13). During the writing phase, the children learned the importance of spelling words correctly and the need to make the layout aesthetically pleasing. Since other classrooms were going to be invited to play in the Health Center, the project group created simple rules to protect their construction. An older child wrote the ideas contributed by younger children. The group approved the final layout of the pamphlet and invitation before they were duplicated and distributed.

Practical Strategy 7:
Encourage Children to Use and
Create References

Learning how to use the simplest form of a dictionary is another literacy milestone for young children.

Figure 4.4 Children learned the value of writing when they received a letter from children in another classroom in answer to their questions about health centers.

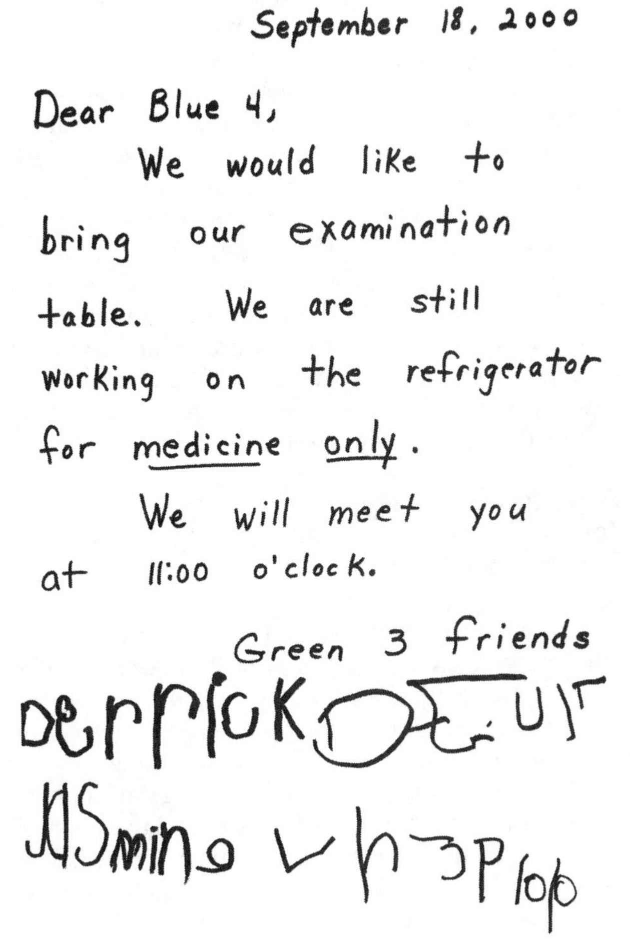

September 18, 2000

Dear Blue 4,
    We would like to bring our examination table. We are still working on the refrigerator for medicine only.
    We will meet you at 11:00 o'clock.

Green 3 friends

oerrioK O£ Uŗ

JASmino ∪h 3P loo

At-risk children may not own a dictionary and may not have easy access to a library to borrow one. When we decided to display our Linden Hill Farm Project in the hallway, the children used a pictionary to create labels with correct spellings for the buildings and animals in the model.

Other teachers have found "word walls" to be very helpful in project work. When frequently used words are displayed at eye level, children can copy the words they might need while writing (Fountas & Pinnell, 1996). As a project develops, new words can be added to the word wall. Using photos to illustrate project words is especially helpful for younger children. During the Farm Project, I placed the vocabulary/photographs on a project time line, which was easily visible to the children.

A videotape of the field experience also serves as a reference. It is useful in building project-related vocabulary, showing the sequence of events during the site visit, or providing additional time to look at objects for sketching and labeling. Individual children can serve as narrators while the group watches the video.

SPEAKING

Practical Strategy 8: Plan for Language-Rich Play

Just as projects create opportunities for meaningful writing, they also create purposes for speaking in the dramatic play that often emerges as part of a project. Rogers and Sawyers (1998) point out that "although play is not a necessary condition for learning language and literacy skills, play is probably the best environment for these abilities to thrive" (p. 64). Play increases the use of oral language. Children use new language as they plan and negotiate their play, which is enriched by project work.

During the Zoo Project, for example, groups of children constructed zoos in the block area during center time and then played with them. Considerable informal discussion occurred. Those who had never been to the zoo had no idea that animals could not be housed on top of the structures, or that farm animals might not be located in the same pens as lions and elephants (see Figure 4.5). Children who had some knowledge of zoos

Figure 4.5 James constructed a zoo during center time; it was made *before* the field-site visit.

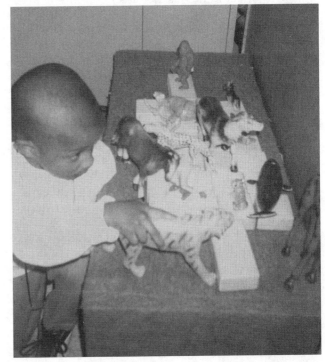

were challenged to communicate with their peers so that the play could proceed according to their frames of reference. Conversation within the group helped some students learn what type of housing was appropriate for each animal. Those who had already visited the zoo used their words to enlighten their peers. These students, who had become the resident resource persons, were asked for advice during later constructions. Thus, the children had opportunities to practice verbal descriptive skills that aid reading development.

Practical Strategy 9:
Encourage Peer Coaching

During project work, children often do peer coaching, which provides another opportunity to practice communication skills. This kind of collaborative work is an effective way to stimulate language development. For example, grouping younger and older children together while sketching at the farm park allowed the older, more verbal children to talk about what they were seeing. In one instance, I observed first-grader Jared telling five-year-old Natasha where to draw the legs of the animal. He even helped her erase her first attempt and pointed to where the legs belonged. The younger child respected Jared's work and accepted his guidance. Another example of peer coaching occurred when Matthew constructed a barn for a different farm project. Once he figured out how to make a pointed roof, he became the "expert" and assisted other children as they built the house and milking parlors. Although his speech was difficult to understand, this unusually quiet kindergartner asserted himself when showing older first graders how to use masking tape and box lids to create the angles of the roof.

Practical Strategy 10:
Help Children Learn How to
Ask Questions

Young children need to learn how to ask questions, and the ability to ask questions in investigation is similar to the skill needed in asking oneself questions in the reading process. Asking questions of others is the forerunner of using silent questioning strategies while reading, such as asking oneself, What do I need to know?, or Is the answer here?

Children often have ideas or comments to share and frequently confuse these statements with questions. In my class, we learn about question words such as *who, what, when, where, why,* and *how.* I guide students in creating questions. For example, consider the following scenario: A child says, "Cows have babies. Babies come out." The intonation in his voice suggests a question. I might reply, "Are you asking how the babies come out?

How the babies are born?" I rephrase the question using a word encountered in our project work. If the child nods, I might say, "How could we find that out?" Suggestions from the children might include looking in our books; asking Mom; saying, "You could tell us"; or asking the expert (the farmer). I might continue, "You could ask the farmer's wife when we go to the farm to tell you about calves being born. You could say, 'How are the babies _____?'" (pausing for the child to finish the sentence). We also learn that question marks indicate to the reader that an answer is needed.

Throughout the course of each project, we learn more about telling and asking questions. As I record the questions that occur throughout the project, I am modeling the correct forms of writing and grammar. The children practice using correct grammar to create a question; they see me writing it and hear it read back to them. In these instances, listening, speaking, writing, and reading are closely intertwined.

Practical Strategy 11:
Tap the Potential of Culminating
Experiences

Culminating experiences in Phase III of project work often provide a multitude of opportunities to develop and practice language and literacy skills. At the conclusion of many projects, the children have created displays in the hallway. For example, we made a candle display as our culminating activity during the Light Project. We invited other classes to our display, and small groups of children explained how the different candles were made. Two children acted as tour guides, explaining how each type of candle was produced. In the Glen Oak Zoo Project, a zoo that had been constructed in our classroom was moved to the hallway, where other classes could enjoy it. Children took turns telling other classes about the zoo and their construction.

At the end of our Bakery Project, we held a bake sale in the bakery we constructed. As children from other classes and adults came to buy baked goods, our children were challenged to use their communication skills to handle the sales. They also had opportunities to explain how they had made the baked goods and built the bakery.

In the Grocery Store Project, each classroom in our wing of the school created a construction in the hallway representing part of the grocery store. When all the parts were complete, two children from each of the five classrooms played in the grocery store each day. Teachers took turns supervising and participating in the dramatic play until all of the children had at least one opportunity to play in the grocery store. Imagine the opportunities for adult-child and child-child communication that this culminating project activity encouraged!

Children from different classrooms also came together for a culminating activity during the Farm Project. Children shared experiences about their farm projects in small multi-age groups. In one area, groups of children used newly learned farm vocabulary to talk informally while they used clay and crayons to create or draw favorite farm animals. In another area, groups read little books about the farm and its animals. At the last station, the group listened to an adult read a big book and then visited and made new friends as they made their "chicken feed" snack together. This provided an opportunity for children to have a conversation with someone from a background or race different from their own. The morning concluded when the entire group reassembled and sang songs about the farm. Language and literacy were enhanced during this relaxing and fun experience.

During the Health Center Project open house, pairs of children took turns acting as hosts, telling about the construction and use of the Health Center. They used newly learned vocabulary such as *examination table, stethoscope,* and *reception desk* as they talked to the audience. Other classes were given a tour of the structure. Visitors coming into the building stopped to listen to the guides, and many became involved in dramatic play with the children.

LISTENING

Practical Strategy 12:
Provide Opportunities to Listen to Experts

Projects provide many opportunities for children to practice listening skills. Their interest and engagement in the investigation motivates them to listen carefully when we visit field sites and experts share information with us. The farmer's wife, the health center nurse, the emergency room nurses who came to our classroom, and the water meter reader who brought in water meters for the project group to examine all helped build experiences and knowledge.

According to Neuman et al. (2000), children learn more from experts when teachers lay the groundwork beforehand. If children generate questions to ask, they are motivated to listen to the answers. When teachers present children's questions to a speaker before a visit, he or she is more likely to address the issues of greatest interest to the children. When listening to a guest speaker talk about a topic of interest to the group, the children have an opportunity to practice listening etiquette (look at the speaker, listen attentively, raise your hand to ask a question, and so forth).

Practical Strategy 13:
Provide Opportunities to Listen to Peers

The class has daily opportunities to listen when we discuss what we will be doing while working on the project. As the group meets and prepares to work, individual members announce plans for the day. At this time they can ask for help with problems they encountered the day before. One child might ask others what they think about his construction or request help in painting or cutting. He might ask his peers where he can go within the school to find materials or information. The group might decide to go to another room to seek answers or solutions to a problem. They may want to record information and listen as the "spellers" in the group help them with words. Members of the project group usually report daily about their project work and may seek help from the entire class to solve a new problem. Collaborative work requires children to continually use and respond to language.

Practical Strategy 14:
Read Topic-Related Informational Books to Children

As we begin to select a topic, I read many topic-related books to the children. These books, both fiction and nonfiction, provide information related to the project and may answer some of our questions or pose additional questions. I go to the public library and select books with good illustrations so that they can be used as references during the project. "By coordinating firsthand experiences with the books made available to them, children gain knowledge, and this knowledge in turn aids their future reading of books" (Schickedanz, 1999, p. 66).

CONCLUSION

Reading, writing, speaking, and listening are literacy components of project work. As previously discussed, the following practical strategies will enhance the benefits of project work and support the development of children's language and literacy skills:

1. Emphasize building vocabulary as a foundation for further learning
2. Encourage children to play around with letter and word recognition
3. Provide opportunities for publishing and reading child-made books
4. Provide events that encourage writing
5. Help children develop e-mail relationships

6. Help children create pamphlets and brochures
7. Encourage children to use and create references
8. Plan for language-rich play
9. Encourage peer coaching
10. Help children learn how to ask questions
11. Tap the potential of culminating experiences
12. Provide opportunities to listen to experts
13. Provide opportunities to listen to peers
14. Read topic-related informational books to children

As illustrated in the following description, project work offers many meaningful opportunities to integrate literacy skills and provides a reason for children to practice them.

THE WATER TO RIVER PROJECT
Jean O'Mara-Thieman

The Water to River Project took place in a multi-age (kindergarten through first grade) classroom at the Valeska Hinton Early Childhood Center, which was described earlier in this chapter. In this urban public school, 53% of the children are from minority families, and 75% qualify as low-income families. The program at Valeska Hinton includes parent involvement and year-round schooling to help meet the needs of these at-risk students. Associate teacher Kendrya' Johnson and student teacher Jaynene Dellitt collaborated with me on this project.

As with children in many other settings, there was great variation in literacy skills among the children in our classroom. Some children did not recognize letters, while others were reading well above their grade level. Some of the children in the class had little previous exposure to books at home. They had not experienced the sophisticated vocabulary sometimes used in non-fiction writing or the long sentences sometimes used in science books. I found that the project approach was very helpful as I dealt with these challenges because it motivated the children to use literacy skills and afforded many opportunities for children at all levels to apply their literacy skills.

PHASE I: BEGINNING THE PROJECT

The original topic for this project was teacher-initiated. It seemed to me that the river would make a good project topic, since our school is very close to the Illinois River. The children would be able to investigate it firsthand. I could also see the potential of this topic to involve all the domains of learning and to meet many curriculum goals.

During Phase I we explored the children's possible interest in various aspects of the river. It took some time before an intense, in-depth investigation developed. Kendrya' and I began the project by sharing some of our memories of the river. We also put out a variety of books and materials related to rivers and responded to children's questions about them (see Figure 4.6).

Figure 4.6 Literacy materials related to rivers were set out on the table to engage the interest of the children.

Figure 4.7 The web that the children started on water reveals how their knowledge moved from the general to scientific concepts, such as evaporation buoyancy.

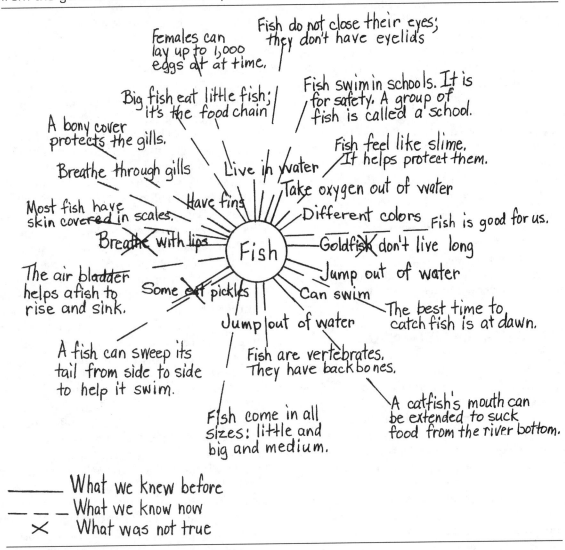

Females can lay up to 1,000 eggs at at time.

Fish do not close their eyes; they don't have eyelids.

Big fish eat little fish; it's the food chain

Fish swim in schools. It is for safety. A group of fish is called a school.

A bony cover protects the gills.

Fish feel like slime. It helps protect them.

Breathe through gills

Live in water

Take oxygen out of water

Most fish have skin covered in scales.

Have fins

Different colors

Fish is good for us.

Breathe with lips

Goldfish don't live long

The air bladder helps a fish to rise and sink.

Some eat pickles

Can swim

Jump out of water

The best time to catch fish is at dawn.

Jump out of water

A fish can sweep its tail from side to side to help it swim.

Fish are vertebrates. They have backbones.

Fish come in all sizes: little and big and medium.

A catfish's mouth can be extended to suck food from the river bottom.

Fish

——— What we knew before
— — — What we know now
✕   What was not true

We read extensively to the children from informational books, such as *What's It Like to Be a Fish?* (Pfeffer & Keller, 1996) and *Who Eats What: Food Chains & Food Webs* (Lauber & Keller, 1995). As we talked with the children, we found that their lexicon of river-related words was very limited, so we began working with them on several lists. For example, we developed a list of fish words that included factual words such as *gills, lateral line, fins, scales,* and *gill slits,* as well as descriptive words such as *wiggly* and *slimy* (PS1: *Emphasize building vocabulary*).

We soon realized that the children had limited prior knowledge of the topic. In fact, some children even said that they had never seen the Illinois River. Perhaps that lack of firsthand experience is the reason they did not seem very interested in the subject. Due to this lack of interest, we decided to rethink the starting point for

our project. Since we knew that all the children had experience with water, we decided to begin with water as the starting point, instead of the less familiar topic of the river. To begin the discussion of this revised topic, we opened the water table and provided the children with opportunities for exploration and guided experimentation with water. We read about water and began a web about the ways that water is used (see Figure 4.7; PS1: *Emphasize building vocabulary*). To assist the children in using vocabulary and writing, I always keep a pile of simply made, small, blank books in the writing area. These blank books have only a few pages, but the children can use them to make as many books as they like; they might write just one or two sentences per book. The children particularly like to take an idea from one of the small books such as *The Storm* (Cowley, 1990) and *Umbrella* (Cowley, 1998) from the Wright Group

Story Box Reading Series and write their own version. For example, in Phase I, when we were searching for ways to interest them in the topic, we featured a book about storms, since it had to do with water.

During Phase I, we were lucky enough to see a puppet show that emphasized the importance of clean drinking water and preventing water pollution. After seeing this show, the children had many questions (PS10: *Help children ask questions*) that reflected their realization that drinking water might come from the river. They had developed a new interest in conserving water and keeping it clean, and it was apparent they were realizing how important water was to their lives. This realization was reflected in the questions they asked:

Are a river and a lake the same thing?
Is there a river in Peoria?
Do we drink water from the river?
What happens if we don't have enough water?
What can we do, or how can we save water?

PHASE II: INVESTIGATION

We responded to the children's questions by providing them with classroom experiences in de-polluting water, but they seemed to be more interested in the idea of water conservation. Much of our water-related vocabulary was developed in the course of experiments. For example, we boiled water to make Jello and learned the words *steam, condensation,* and *absorption* (PS1: *Emphasize building vocabulary*). Experiments like this were often set up as learning center activities, and I posted big recipe charts to help guide the activity. Symbols helped the children decipher the text (PS2: *Encourage playing with letters and words*).

We continued to plan experiences that would expand the children's awareness of water and spark in-depth project work. For example, we planned a field-site visit to the local lock and dam on the Illinois River in East Peoria. I made a preliminary visit to the lock and dam two weeks in advance of our field trip and took pictures of what the children might see there. We loaded these pictures onto the computer and labeled them so that the children could view them during choice time (PS7: *Encourage using references*). I think exposure to these pictures helped the children develop good questions to ask on the day of the visit (PS10: *Help children ask questions*). Our guide at the lock and dam was Mr. Moss, from the Army Corps of Engineers (PS12: *Provide opportunities to listen to experts*). He talked about the proper care of the river and the animals that live in it. The children developed questions before the trip:

Do barges carry people?
Why are there lids on the barges?
Why is the tugboat so long?
Where do the barges come from?

As Mr. Moss answered the children's questions, he stressed that all of us need to take care of the Illinois River and emphasized the important role the river plays in the balance of nature and the lives of human beings.

Since some of the children had never been to the Illinois River and had no idea about all the activity that takes place there, they were fascinated by the rushing water, the movement of the boats and barges, and the bridges. They were surprised by the amount of trash that had built up along the edges of the river, the erosion of the riverbank, and the dirtiness of the river. The sheer size and closeness of the barges to the lock and dam was amazing, as was the amount of water that rushed into and receded from the locks.

The children used their clipboards to draw and write notes at the field site (see Figure 4.8). When we returned, they used their notes as a reference for more writing. We always take time to write and share about our experience when we return from a field trip. Later, they revised and edited their notes for a class resource book (PS4: *Encourage writing*). We also make sure that the children have time each day to write in their journals. Often, on the day following our field-site visits, the children write personal reflections about the visit in their journals. I help them by modeling for the large group with some sample sentences. I also work with individual children as needed (PS4: *Encourage writing*).

The boys and girls wrote descriptions to accompany the pictures we took on our field-site visit. Many of the children dictated their descriptions to one of the teachers as she typed them into the word processor (PS4: *Encourage writing*). The pictures and descriptions were posted around the classroom to use as references for discussion and drawing (PS7: *Encourage using references*). Other field sketches (see Figure 4.9) and samples of information collected on the trip were placed in a class book for reading and reference or in individual children's folders. A picture album of the trip was also created.

In the days following the field trip, we brainstormed methods for saving water and challenged the students to try some of these methods at home. For example, they tried turning off the water while brushing their teeth and used a tally to record the number of times they did it in a week. We also experimented with water conservation at school during breakfast, lunch, and snack. They tried to turn off the water more frequently when washing their hands and to rinse their dishes more quickly. During one of our discussions about water, a student suggested that we make posters or

Figure 4.8 The girls sketch the East Peoria lock and dam. Reviewing pictures of the lock and dam helped them think about what information they wanted to collect.

write letters to other classrooms about saving water (PS6: *Help children create brochures*). The children were very enthusiastic about the idea of sharing their new knowledge with other students, and this became the big challenge in Phase II. I recognized this as a wonderful way for children to develop and apply their speaking and literacy skills (PS11: *Tap culminating experiences*).

The children developed three main areas of interest during Phase II. The first area centered on the children's enduring interest in clean water. They continued to read books about keeping water clean (see Figure 4.10), and we viewed a movie on this subject. In keeping with their idea of informing other classes about clean water, the children wrote a letter to the other students in the school. They also designed and made posters about clean water (PS11: *Tap culminating experiences*). In order to decide what to write in the letters and on the posters, students met in small discussion groups. They listened and responded to each other's ideas (PS9: *Encourage peer coaching;* PS13: *Provide opportunities to listen to peers*). They then developed posters for classroom presentations and later posted them in places where other students might use water, such as the school restrooms and near water fountains (PS6: *Help children create brochures*). The children effectively communicated their ideas through print.

The second interest developed during Phase II was fish. All of the children shared in some aspects of this thread of the investigation, but a subgroup continued on into a deeper investigation. The discussion of fish

Figure 4.9 A first grader's representational drawing of East Peoria lock and dam. Note the boat moving through the lock in the upper-right-hand corner.

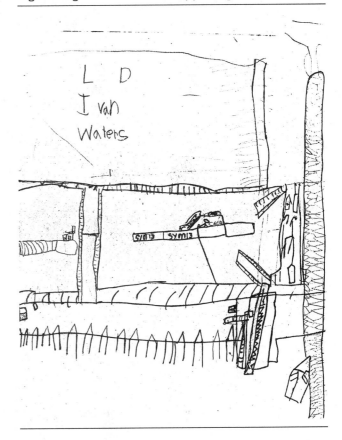

Figure 4.10 The boys research information on clean water to share with other classes.

began when the children were able to examine a real fish. They also learned more about fish by drawing the fish in a large tank near the school entryway (see Figure 4.11). We purchased a fish tank for the classroom at this time, and many of the children in the class helped to prepare it. The children read books about fish and prepared small written reports about types of fish (PS7: *Encourage using references*), and several children wrote "diamond" poems about fish (PS8: *Plan language-rich play*). For example, Nehemiah wrote

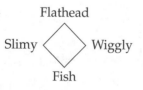

Flathead

Slimy ◇ Wiggly

Fish

Many children painted and drew fish, and, ultimately, a small group worked together to create a realistic representation of a large-mouthed bass. They wanted to be sure that all parts of the fish were included and accurately placed, and I was delighted to see them use diagrams that they located in an encyclopedia for this purpose (PS7: *Encourage using references*). While some students wandered in and out of this construction, a core group of four students stuck with it from beginning to end. Ivan drew the original, small

outline, and then the group helped him to use the overhead projector to enlarge and outline it. The children tried several different materials to make the fish three-dimensional, and they struggled with the problem of how to represent the scales and gills. They tried different coverings and determined that bubble wrap would work best to represent scales. Two members of this group made a presentation to the class about what they had learned about bass and the story of the construction of the giant bass.

The students showed cooperation in both large and small group settings as they worked on the River Proj-

Figure 4.11 Time 1 and Time 2 drawings of fish by a girl. The growth in her understanding of fish is represented in the details, proportions, and placement of the features in the second fish drawing.

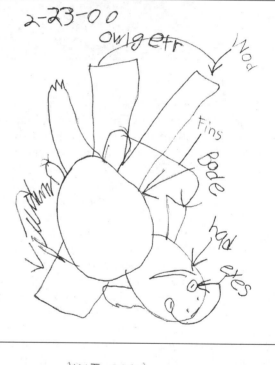

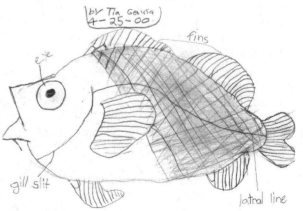

Figure 4.12 One of many elaborate bridges built in the block area during the Water to River Project.

ect. Each of them seemed to understand that sometimes they needed to step up and take leadership or responsibility for an activity so that their group could complete what it had set out to accomplish. The four children who were most intensely involved with constructing the fish took turns with the work that needed to be done. A particular child seemed to take the lead when his or her individual talents were required. For example, Ivan drew well, so he drew the original fish (PS11: *Tap culminating experiences*).

The third thread that the children investigated during Phase II was bridges. The class had traveled across a bridge to visit the lock and dam in East Peoria. Although many of the children had crossed this bridge before, they became more interested in and aware of bridges once they started their investigation of the river. This interest was reflected in the constructions of bridges that began to emerge in the block area. At first, these were very basic constructions, but their complexity grew as the children participated in activities that helped them explore different types of bridges (see Figure 4.12). We heard them using a number of bridge and water vocabulary words as they talked with each other about their constructions. We were really impressed with the richness of their vocabulary as their bridges became more and more elaborate (PS8: *Plan language-rich play*).

Additional complex structures emerged in the block area as the children added more details to their bridges with LEGOS, K-Nex, popsicle sticks, and paper. I taught one small multi-age group of children to build bridges with K-Nex by looking at the K-nex diagrams and then relating them to the different pieces (see Figure 4.13). It was fascinating to see these children become the teachers and mentors for other children in the class as they wanted to learn to use the K-Nex (PS9: *Encourage peer coaching*).

Figure 4.13 A group of children completes a suspension bridge they made with K-Nex.

Figure 4.14 Several children wrote a book about fish and illustrated their cover.

The children truly worked together in the block area, discussing and agreeing on how to proceed with the constructions. If the bridges worked, the children knew immediately. If they did not, they also knew immediately, had further discussion, and made adjustments (PS9: *Encourage peer coaching*). There were many opportunities for problem solving as they worked to build bridges (PS8: *Plan language-rich play*).

In Phase II, the children's homemade books were more often about the information they had acquired (see Figure 4.14) rather than the adaptation of someone else's book. Though the books were still very brief, the children would visit the vocabulary lists or the word wall to find the words they needed to express themselves (PS7: *Encourage using references*; PS3: *Provide opportunities for publishing*). What was even more exciting to me was when they used reference books to find the words they needed (PS14: *Read books*).

PHASE III: CONCLUDING THE PROJECT

The Water to River Project slowly wound down in the spring. The children often reflected on their investigation in their journals. In the beginning, their comments or reflections simply stated what they liked about the activities, but as their expertise grew, they became more observant. The way they wrote about their learning reflected their level of understanding. For example, a few children could write a detailed entry about the complete food chain, while others wrote about their realization that big fish ate smaller fish (PS4: *Encourage writing*).

As a culminating piece of work, the children created a display in the hallway near the entrance to our building (see Figure 4.15). The display was separated

Figure 4.15 The hallway display in Phase III included drawings, paintings, and descriptions that explained what the children had learned. Note the Time 1 and Time 2 webs at the top of the display.

into two sections: one depicted a clean water environment that featured fish and other water animals, and the other section showed a dirty water environment. The children were able to incorporate many of the items they had already made, including posters, paintings, constructions, stories, and photographs. They documented what they had learned by writing their own captions for many of the items they chose for the display (PS7: *Encourage using references*). Their understanding of the usefulness of predicting, observing, comparing, investigating, and drawing conclusions was apparent in the display. It also revealed how the children's disposition to make this world a good place in which to live grew through this experience. In general, this project seemed to open their eyes to the idea that the environment belongs to every one of us, and what we do as individuals has an impact on everyone else. Many visitors to our building looked at the children's work, read their documentation, and noted their concern for water and the river.

TEACHER REFLECTIONS

Since this was only my second project, it was a big undertaking for me. However, it was rewarding to see the children truly engaged in learning. Their thinking, creative ideas, focus, and in-depth study impressed me. It was interesting to see various students take leadership roles and encourage other children to become involved and try new things. It was certainly rewarding to observe peers teaching, sharing, researching, and solving problems with others. I saw how well the project experiences correlated with state goals and district curriculum objectives, and how our assessment system, Work Sampling, allowed children to demonstrate in a variety of ways the knowledge and skills gained during the project. A project that started with a topic that might typically be considered "science" expanded to incorporate all domains as the students researched and executed their ideas. For example, the children applied a broad spectrum of literacy skills and strategies, including letter writing, map reading, creating and using resource information, writing on the computer, communicating with others through discussions, speaking, and listening. In addition, it was encouraging to see the children maintain their interest and enthusiasm right up until the last week of school.

As a teacher, I developed a better understanding about how projects work and strategies for getting chil-

dren involved. I learned how enjoyable it is to be a colearner with your students and that in order to create an environment where children are eager to learn, it is important to encourage students to take a leadership role in determining the direction of the project. I became more aware of my role as a teacher, and I now recognize the need to further develop the questioning skills that help children to be more insightful. Putting into practice what I have read about the project approach continues to help me develop a deeper understanding of how the process works and its many benefits.

REFERENCES

Adams, M. J. (1990). *Beginning to read: Thinking and learning about print.* Cambridge, MA: MIT Press.

Au, K. (1993). *Literacy instruction in multicultural settings.* New York: Harcourt Brace.

Bruner. (1996). *The culture of education.* Cambridge, MA: Harvard University.

Burns, M. S., Griffin, P., & Snow, C. E. (Eds.). (1999). *Starting out right: A guide to promoting children's reading success.* Washington, DC: National Academy Press.

Cowley, J. (1990). *The storm.* Bethel, WA: Wright Group/McGraw-Hill.

Cowley, J. (1998). *Umbrella.* Bethel, WA: Wright Group/McGraw-Hill.

Fountas, I. C., & Pinnell, G. S. (1996). *Guided reading: Good first teaching for all children.* Portsmouth, NH: Heinemann.

Helm, J. H., & Katz, L. (2001). *Young investigators: The project approach in the early years.* New York: Teachers College Press.

Lauber, P., & Keller, H. (1995). *Who eats what: Food chains & food webs.* Reading, MA: Scott Foresman.

Meier, D. R. (2000). *Scribble scrabble: Learning to read and write.* New York: Teachers College Press.

Neuman, S. B., Copple, C., & Bredekamp, S. (2000). *Learning to read and write: Developmentally appropriate practices for young children.* Washington, DC: National Association for the Education of Young Children.

Pfeffer, W., & Keller, H. (1996). *What's it like to be a fish?* New York: HarperCollins.

Rogers, C. S., & Sawyers, J. K. (1998). *Play in the lives of children.* Washington, DC: National Association for the Education of Young Children.

Schickedanz, J. A. (1999). *Much more than the ABCs: The early stages of reading and writing.* Washington, DC: National Association for the Education of Young Children.

Snow, C. E., Burns, M. S., & Griffin, P. (Eds.). (1998). *Preventing reading difficulties in young children.* Washington, DC: National Academy Press.

CHAPTER 5

Responding to Children's Special Needs

Contributors: Judy Harris Helm, Sallee Beneke, Pam Scranton, and Sharon Doubet

DEFINING THE CHALLENGE
Judy Harris Helm and Sallee Beneke

In recent years, there has been a growing trend to "educate and include" children who have been identified with special needs in general preschool and child care programs (Shonkoff & Meisels, 2000, p. 10). Section 612 of the Individuals with Disabilities Education Act (IDEA) requires that to the extent possible services for preschool children be located in the least restrictive environment (Wolery & Odom, 2000). Those who value inclusion "support the right of all children, regardless of their abilities, to participate actively in natural settings within their communities" (Sandall, McLean, & Smith, 2000, p. 150) and believe that this type of learning and care environment will be most effective in educating children with special needs (Klein & Gilkerson, 2000). In 1997–98, 75% of the more than 5.5 million 6- through 21-year-olds with disabilities served under IDEA were educated in regular classrooms with their nondisabled peers (U.S. Department of Education, 2000).

The criteria that qualify children as having special needs vary from state to state (Shonkoff & Meisels, 2000). Children with special needs are classified into one of thirteen categories of disabilities to establish their eligibility for early intervention and special education services. "Because of the detrimental effects of early labeling, IDEA allows states to use the category 'developmental delay' for young children with special needs" (Wolery & Wilbers, 1994, pp. 4–5).

All children who receive special education services must have an Individual Education Plan (IEP). This plan identifies individual goals and objectives for the child and the services he or she will receive through the school. Parents are required to be included in the team that develops the IEP, as first mandated in 1975 by the Education for All Handicapped Act (Public Law 94-142). Other members of the team include teachers, caregivers, and educational and medical specialists who may be involved in the child's education.

Children with special needs benefit when they are integrated into the kinds of programs that they might attend if they were not disabled. To be successful, however, some children with specific disabilities require adaptation of the curriculum or the classroom environment. Teachers need up-to-date information on the specific special needs of the child and how to meet those needs. In some cases, additional staff must be provided. Whether or not the inclusion of a child with special needs into a regular education classroom is successful may depend on the teacher's ability to adapt the curriculum and integrate the child into the social life of the classroom.

In general, classrooms that include play, opportunities for self-initiation, and activities that promote all developmental areas are beneficial for children with special needs, just as they are for typically developing children. In fact, it may be even more important to find strategies that capitalize on children's interest "for children at lower developmental levels with more significant disabilities in which the capacity for generalization and transfer of learning is more limited" (Klein & Gilkerson, 2000, p. 457). Because good early childhood classrooms take advantage of the natural inclination of young children to be curious and active learners, they tend to be organized into learning centers or areas where children can choose from a number of activities or materials. The better the classroom environment, the more involved teachers are in cognitive play with children (Farran, 2000, p. 528). Open-ended materials and materials that can be used to teach a variety of skills at a variety of levels are often part of these centers. The teacher can expand the range of difficulty in the learning that occurs in an area through the questions she asks and the modeling she uses as she interacts with the children. Most young children have short attention spans and do not respond well in long, large-group activities such as long circle times or whole-group completion of worksheets. For this reason, it is more effective to provide many teacher-directed learning experiences individually or in small groups. Individualized goals and objectives are more easily incorporated into this type of teaching.

When these typical approaches to providing learning experiences in a classroom do not meet the specific needs of a child, they can be adapted or expanded to accommodate the child's individual needs:

The purpose of an adaptation is to assist children in compensating for intellectual, physical, or behavioral challenges. They allow children to use their current skills while promoting the acquisition of new skills. Adaptations can make the difference between a child merely being present in the class and a child being actively involved. (*Accommodating all Children in the Early Childhood Classroom*, 1999)

However, adapting learning experiences is a new skill for many teachers, especially those in child care and preschool environments.

Children with special needs also often require special support and services, and teachers have concerns about how these supports will be provided. "Inclusive education involves a commitment to every child, and every child requires different supports for learning" (Villa et al., 1995, p. 139). When the team meets to plan the child's IEP, they may decide that additional staff will be in the classroom on a daily basis, or that specialists should regularly work with the child in the classroom. Integrating additional staff members and activities into the classroom requires flexibility and skill in collaboration.

An important component of an educational program for children with special needs is involvement in a community of learners. Classrooms in which the development of a caring community is a priority are beneficial for all children and even more so for children with special needs. Children are more likely to risk trying something new or to stick with a difficult task when they feel safe and accepted. They are motivated to participate and work to the best of their abilities when the work is related to their classroom community. Teachers of children with special needs are able to model accep-

tance of a child's disability and to spotlight the strengths of the child and his or her contributions to the class. In this way, all children develop appreciation for one another and learn how to respond positively to people with disabilities.

We have observed that responding to children's special needs/diverse learning styles presents some unique challenges for the early childhood professional. These challenges include

- Providing a developmentally appropriate environment for all children
- Planning experiences that are both teacher initiated and child initiated
- Developing adaptations to meet diverse learning styles and physical needs
- Writing developmentally appropriate IEP goals and meeting those goals
- Conducting ongoing authentic assessment

Children with special needs are usually better served in inclusive settings. Training in adapting curriculum and environments, creating an active classroom, making a flexible schedule, and developing useful teaching strategies can help teachers successfully include children with special needs in their classrooms.

PRACTICAL STRATEGIES
Pam Scranton and Sharon Doubet

Natalie and Jared sat side by side on the ground sketching the horse (see Figure 5.1). Both visited McGlothlin Farm Park as part of the Farm Project. Natalie, a preschooler, was becoming frustrated because she could not make her drawing look like the living horse in front of her. Jared, her first-grade friend, put his arm around her and guided her through this challenging drawing activity. "Natalie, you have to put the body first, then you put the legs on. Then you put the tail on his bottom. See how he has sticking up ears?" Natalie listened intently to Jared's descriptions and hesitantly began to sketch her horse. After she finished her sketch, she ran up with her clipboard and proudly exclaimed, "Teacher, look what me and Jared did!"

Natalie was one of 18 students in a preschool class that included children with many diverse learning styles. She was diagnosed with Fetal Alcohol Syndrome at birth, and as a result of a full case study, she had been placed in an inclusive setting, as required by IDEA. Her IEP included goals in speech and language, fine and gross motor skills, cognitive development, and social and emotional growth. On that spring day at the Farm Park, Jared's support created a bridge that helped Natalie draw the horse they were observing. In the

Figure 5.1 Natalie and Jared sketch a horse.

course of the project work, Natalie met several goals in all four domains of her IEP.

Over the last six years we have been working together to explore the use of the project approach for children with special needs. As teachers who include project work in our curriculum, we know that all children benefit from investigating and exploring the world in an authentic way. The project approach moves each child forward on his or her individual developmental continuum. Thus, the project approach is especially useful to teachers of children with special needs, because it helps them respect children's developmental levels.

In attempting to increase learning opportunities for children with special needs in project work and help them practice the skills identified as their IEP goals, we have found certain strategies to be practical and useful. Examples of project experiences from our classrooms are provided in the description of each practical strategy to demonstrate how the project approach can support their implementation with diverse learners. We have chosen to organize our discussion according to the development domains used in setting IEP goals: speech and language development; cognitive development; social and emotional development; fine motor development; and gross motor development.

SPEECH AND LANGUAGE DEVELOPMENT

Practical Strategy 1:
Encourage Participation in Small-Group Discussions

Practical Strategy 2:
Promote Increased Vocabulary Knowledge and Use

Encouraging language development is a goal for most early childhood educators, not just those who work with children with special needs. Many of the children we see in inclusive classrooms have speech and language disabilities and language goals in their IEPs. Important communication goals for children with disabilities include child-to-child and adult-to-child interactions (Wolery & Odom, 2000). Both of these important types of interactions occur naturally in project work.

All three phases of project work promote language development through the literacy activities of reading, writing, listening, and speaking. During Phase I activities, children participate in making lists, recording questions, and webbing. They watch as the teacher models the writing process or helps others record information on their clipboards. For instance, during the Grocery Store Project, Cody helped compile the list of items needed for the children's construction of a grocery store. Cody has Aspberger's Syndrome and has difficulty retrieving words as he speaks. As the children verbally named items, Pam wrote them down on chart paper for later transcribing. This activity allowed Cody to practice labeling everyday items in his environment, a goal on his IEP. The only adaptation needed was to give him some books with pictures of vocabulary words as visual cues during the list making.

During Phase II, children represent what they are learning, and several different types of language activities typically take place. Often children will attempt to label crucial parts of sketches by referring to the word wall or informational books, asking an adult for help, or writing phonetically. They write questions for expert visitors and record the answers by either drawing or writing. If constructions are part of the representations, children will often make signs that identify parts of them or inform another group of children of the work in progress. Diagramming and graphing information during investigations is another language/literacy activity that may happen in Phase II work.

Cody was a member of the project group that visited a grocery store during Phase II of the Grocery Store Project. During the site visit, the children were respon-

Figure 5.2 Meeting IEP goals in speech and language development.

Sample IEP Goals	Examples of a Child's Experiences During Project Work
Goal 1. Engages in communication during classroom activities	• Attends to small-group discussion to determine project topic • Forms interview questions for visiting experts in a project group • Participates in small-group discussion listing items needed for construction
Goal 2. Increases vocabulary	• Engages in development of the project word wall • Uses new words to label drawings • Incorporates learned vocabulary into project discussion with adults and children • Uses appropriate terminology during second and third webbing experiences

sible for diagramming the layout of the IGA grocery store and labeling the bakery, meat department, and dairy department on the diagram. With his clipboard and an adult volunteer's support, Cody participated by drawing the different departments. While the volunteer labeled each section when he was finished, Cody still had to plan where each department's representation would be placed on his paper, and he had to tell the name of each department to the adult. Taking part in the project helped him work on the IEP goals related to labeling.

In Phase III, children seek to share their learning with others, and language activities include making books, labeling exhibits, or writing invitations for an open house. As children began playing in the grocery store constructions they had developed in Phase II of the Grocery Store Project, the students in the classroom across the hall from us were intrigued. As they watched the children in Pam's class playing in their construction day after day, they lingered in the door of their own classroom with expectant faces, hoping for an invitation to play. Cody was part of a small group that wrote an invitation asking the other class to view their grocery store and play in it. The children made suggestions for the wording of the invitation as Pam recorded their ideas on the computer. The invitations were written in a few minutes, and a copy was printed out for delivery to the other class. Cody observed as his words were written down, and the important connection between written and spoken language was reinforced. This was not only a goal on his IEP, but it was also part of the assessment system for the class as a whole. Samples of children's IEP goals in the area of speech and language and examples of the kinds of project work experiences that might help children meet these goals are included in Figure 5.2.

COGNITIVE DEVELOPMENT

Practical Strategy 3:
Engage Children in Intellectual Thinking by Supporting Their Investigation of a High-Interest Topic

Practical Strategy 4:
Support Children in Transferring and Representing New Information

The project approach offers many opportunities for growth and assessment in the cognitive domain. As children become interested in a topic, they think about it, become intellectually engaged, and strive to remember what they have seen and heard. They see reasons for using academic skills such as measuring, classifying, counting, labeling, diagramming, and graphing. Their interest inspires them to use their imaginations and think creatively. As they strengthen their dispositions to be curious and to investigate, they develop a fuller and deeper sense of their environments and experiences. We specifically look for children to attempt to make sense of an experience; theorize, analyze, and hypothesize; make and check predictions; strive for accuracy; persist in seeking solutions to problems; and speculate about cause and effect relationships. The types of cognitive activities often found in a project range from recalling information, to organizing it for reporting, to problem solving. For example, children might use creative thinking to determine how to use a spring as part of a construction. When children are engaged in project work, they build high-level cognitive skills. As they learn about the topic, they remember what they have experienced and what they have seen and heard, and they develop a knowledge base for further project work.

Figure 5.3 Meeting IEP goals in cognitive development.

Sample IEP Goals	Examples of a Child's Experiences During Project Work
Goal 1. Organizes and repeats new information	• Sequences a series of photographs to tell the story of a field-site visit • Participates in graphing information during a field-site visit • Charts information learned through observation
Goal 2. Chooses tools to use for investigation	• Chooses appropriate tools for specific investigation (magnifying glass to enlarge ants) • Shares learning with others after an investigation

During the Vet Project, Cherise was involved in building the veterinarian's office. She was four years old and had an IEP that included several cognitive goals. As she was building the "holding cage," several of the children challenged her decision to build the cardboard bars on the outside of the cage. Cherise ran to get a photo of the holding cage and ran back to the construction site in the classroom, yelling, "See, the real one gots the bars on the outside too! That's cause the doggies won't get cut." Cherise had just demonstrated information recall, represented what she had learned through her construction, and given us a valuable insight into how she was learning and thinking. In that quick, five-minute interlude, we had also gained some assessment information for Cherise's IEP and Work Sampling System checklist (Edmiaston, 1998).

Project work emphasizes children's interests, which is particularly important in engaging some children with special needs in cognitive learning experiences (Edmiaston, 1998). As project teachers it is important for us to watch for children's interests—by looking for their facial expressions to change and their fascination and persistence with project materials to emerge—and then help them expand on their explorations.

In Figure 5.3 we have provided examples of IEP goals related to cognitive development that are typically experienced during project work. These examples provide only a glimpse of possible natural opportunities that children may experience in project work that support IEPs.

SOCIAL AND EMOTIONAL DEVELOPMENT

Practical Strategy 5:
Increase Opportunities for Collaborative Work and Problem Solving

Collaborative work during a project is very important and occurs throughout the process as children lis-ten to each other and work together to achieve their goals. Through project work, children learn to respect each other's ideas, and a classroom community is created. Rebecca Edmiaston (1998) reported in her study of project work in an inclusive classroom that projects build a community within the building where no one is different and no one is excluded. Both children and teachers learn and develop in this accepting environment. While engaged in project work, children listen to and respect each other, and they often make adaptations for their friends who have special needs. For example, children in Pam's classroom often brought Billy his therapy chair when he needed it, or remembered that Emily needed her stool to reach the easel and retrieved it for her. Project work encourages this type of social and emotional growth as children learn to work together.

During the Bird Project, which is described in the next part of this chapter, five-year-old Brandon became involved in constructing an eagle. Brandon's IEP included several social and emotional goals, and he came from an extremely at-risk home environment. He had a hard time identifying his feelings, dealing with anger, and playing cooperatively with friends. The eagle we had observed during the Wildlife Prairie Park visit greatly interested Brandon, and he came up with the idea to construct an eagle of his own. The first day he began working on the Styrofoam body, two other children became interested and wanted to join him. Brandon proclaimed, "You can't, it was my idea!" The other two children asked for our help, and we approached Brandon with the thought that they could offer assistance and more ideas about how to build the eagle. Professionals need to encourage children to help each other (Sandall et al., 2000). Reluctantly, Brandon allowed them to participate, and a small project group was formed. Each day the three boys worked together—with some conflicts and problem solving along the way—but in the end they built a replica of the brown eagle they had investigated. Through this experience,

Figure 5.4 Meeting IEP goals in social and emotional development.

Sample IEP Goals	Examples of a Child's Experiences During Project Work
Goal 1. Works collaboratively with others	• Participates in planning surveys • Constructs play environments with others • Develops ability to take turns while asking questions during a field-site visit
Goal 2. Uses problem-solving skills and vocabulary	• Chooses to use language during a project • As play begins in the project environment, engages in discussing the process of taking turns

Brandon grew in his ability to work with other children and solve problems during a conflict; both were social and emotional goals on his IEP. Sample IEP goals in social and emotional development and project work experiences that can help children meet these goals are listed in Figure 5.4.

FINE MOTOR SKILLS

Practical Strategy 6:
Support the Daily Use of Writing and Art Tools for a Purpose

Project work offers many opportunities for children to practice and strengthen their fine motor skills. During project work, children draw, write, graph, glue, tape, cut, build, and paint in order to represent what they are learning. They become excited about sharing their new knowledge, and their reluctance to use fine motor skills is often overridden by the desire to share what they have experienced.

Billy, a five-year-old with occupational and physical therapy goals, participated in class activities for the first time during the Bird Project. He has cerebral palsy and had previously avoided activities that required him to draw, write, or paint. During Phase II work of the Bird Project, Billy became fascinated with the physical diagrams of birds that he found in an informational book. After several days of looking in the books, running his hands over the diagrams, and naming parts of the bird's body, Billy was persuaded to pick up a clipboard and pencil. His first attempt at sketching consisted of a large circle shape with lines coming out of it, which represented the lines Pam typically used to label the parts of the children's drawings. Billy was drawing! He came back to this activity day after day and drew several different examples of bird diagrams. By the second week, Billy was satisfied with his drawings, but he would not attempt to label the parts on those important lines he

had drawn. Pam labeled the parts for him the first time, and later Billy used this example of writing to label his own copy. Soon he was copying words right off the project word wall onto his diagram! During the Bird Project, Billy became more comfortable with pencils, markers, and pens, but, more importantly, he became a writer and drawer. His IEP goals in the area of fine motor skills were met through an important classroom strategy: interaction with materials, children, and adults (Sandall et al., 2000). Further examples of experiences children are likely to have in project work that support IEP goals in fine motor skills are listed in Figure 5.5.

GROSS MOTOR SKILLS

Practical Strategy 7:
Provide Opportunities for Gross Motor Skill Development Within Classroom Activities

The physical development of young children should be considered throughout the learning environment and across the curriculum (Bredekamp & Copple, 1997). During project work, children have the opportunity to use their large muscles to interact with the environment on a field-site visit. Later they use their large muscles in constructing representations of what they observed. Many challenges to motor planning and many opportunities to practice repetitive tasks occur naturally in project work.

In Phase II of the Playground Project, four-year-old Carmen was part of the group that built an environmental playground out of scrap materials. Carmen was diagnosed with cerebral palsy and had many gross motor goals on her IEP, including walking on a balance beam. The children were working on the smooth surface of our classroom patio with scrap materials, including several planks. As the group kept rearranging the planks, someone discovered the concept of incline and

Figure 5.5 Meeting IEP goals in fine motor skills.

Sample IEP Goals	Examples of a Child's Experiences During Project Work
Goal 1. Incorporates writing and art tools into daily classroom activities	• Engages in observational drawing • Labels pictures and drawings • Uses writing tools to record information • Participates in painting to represent learning
Goal 2. Increases ability to use pincer grasp during centers/project time	• Tears materials in preparation for construction • Models with clay to represent learning • Cuts materials for construction purposes

supported the planks at the top to make a slide. They began walking up and down the inclined plank and looking for things to roll down it. Pam watched carefully, hoping that Carmen would attempt to walk on the plank, too. Quietly Pam moved the plank down to the level ground again and watched as Carmen walked on the flat plank again and again! As the other three children came back with their rubber balls for rolling, Carmen was still walking on her "balance beam." Her IEP goal had been met through exploration with scrap materials during project work. This experience also illustrates a recommendation by the Division of Early Childhood of the Council for Exceptional Children to use teaching strategies and adaptations that promote the child's participation in classroom activities (Sandall et al., 2000). Figure 5.6 contains a sample gross motor IEP goal and several examples of supportive experiences that often take place during project work.

COMMON QUESTIONS AND ANSWERS

As we have spoken with other teachers about the benefits of using the project approach with children with special needs, we have been asked many questions. In this section, we provide answers to several of the most commonly asked questions.

Can young children who are nonverbal or low functioning be involved in project work?

Project work is an appropriate approach when working with children who have a variety of developmental levels, because each child enters the work at their level of understanding and progresses from that point. If the topic of the project is potatoes, a teacher may have one child who knows that we eat potatoes and another child who knows that there are many varieties of potatoes and that they grow in dirt. Clearly, those two children will experience the Potato Project in their own developmental fashion. The advantage of this collaborative approach is that the child who has more information about potatoes will help the other child learn more about the topic. When working with children who are not verbalizing their knowledge, teachers are forced to become very observant. They must watch the child's face and body language for excitement, intensity, and general responses to their work.

How can I use the project approach in a self-contained classroom with no peer models?

While integrated classroom settings are typically most successful in meeting children's needs, project work is also rewarding in segregated settings. Even in

Figure 5.6 Meeting an IEP goal in gross motor skills.

Sample IEP Goals	Examples of a Child's Experiences During Project Work
Goal 1. Increase upper body strength	• Stacks large blocks during construction of a play environment • Loads, transports, and unloads materials for construction • Holds an object in place for hammering • Engages in repetitive movement required for sawing • Holds arms in place while attaching pieces to a construction

a typical, self-contained, early childhood classroom for children with special needs, the students will be at a variety of developmental levels. In the beginning of a project, the children will probably rely more on the teacher as a model, but some of the higher functioning children will naturally take over this role.

How can I meet IEP goals within the project?

If the IEP goals are developmentally appropriate, they can be met within the project with a little planning by the teacher. Small-group work during a project is also an opportunity to work on IEP goals, and teachers can organize the group work to incorporate goals for individual children.

CONCLUSION

Project work is one approach we have found to be successful in classrooms with diverse learners. When responding to children's special needs, a teacher considers each child's developmental levels and what should be learned next and then plans activities to move the child forward on the learning continuum.

Many important strategies for teaching children with special needs are supported by project work. These strategies include

1. Encourage participation in small-group discussions
2. Promote increased vocabulary knowledge and use
3. Engage children in intellectual thinking by supporting their investigation of a high-interest topic
4. Support children in transferring and representing new information
5. Increase opportunities for collaborative work and problem solving
6. Support the daily use of writing and art tools for a purpose
7. Provide opportunities for gross motor skill development within classroom activities

As shown in the description of the Bird Project below, during project work children are involved in planning and implementing these strategies as active participants in the learning process. As they become engaged in a project, the children express interest in a topic and tell what they know about it and what they want to know. Together the group decides how they will find out the answers to their questions and represent their learning. Observation of children through each of these steps gives teachers the opportunity to assess their growth without disrupting the children's involvement in active, engaged, meaningful learning. This should be a goal in educating all children.

THE BIRD PROJECT
Pam Scranton

The Bird Project took place in the Bright Beginnings multi-age prekindergarten classroom in the Congerville-Eureka-Goodfield School District. The district (based on the Illinois School Report Card) is in an isolated, rural area and provides no public transportation; 29% of the students are eligible for free/reduced price lunch, and 7.8% come from low-income families. The mobility rate is 8.7%, and 97.8% of the students are white. Both children with identified special needs and children who have been identified as meeting at-risk criteria are enrolled in the Bright Beginnings program. Twenty children were enrolled in the half-day class, and classroom space was shared with a Head Start program. Associate teacher Ellen Griffin collaborated with me on this project.

Project work has helped me respond to the special needs of children in my classroom. As I have become more experienced in project work, I have learned how useful this approach can be in encouraging children with special needs to become involved in the life of the classroom and in applying knowledge, skills, and dispositions that are identified as goals in each child's IEP.

There is strong support for teachers to do project work in the Bright Beginnings program. When I felt I needed an extra set of adult hands, I often had parent volunteers. Many of these parents had come to understand the value of project work through their older children who had been in my class. In fact, some of the parents had been with me for several years, and I had built strong, positive relationships with them. Even though project work was not part of these parents' own childhood experiences, they had come to recognize how effective it was in teaching their children. We were also lucky to have money available for extra project materials and field trip transportation. The administration of the Bright Beginnings program was also supportive. They value teachers as learners, support professional development, and encouraged me as I continued to learn how to use the project approach.

While the curriculum in our class is developed in response to the interests of the children, we are also careful to be sure that we meet the benchmarks of the Illinois Early Learning Standards. We evaluate children on an ongoing basis with the Work Sampling System, which helps us to assess each child's progress and performance. In combination, the standards and curriculum-embedded assessment assure us that we are serving all our children well.

At the time the Bird Project took place, three children with special needs were enrolled in my class, and two of them became deeply involved in the project. As introduced earlier in this chapter, Brandon, a five-year-old, met the criteria for a behavior disorder. Jason, a three-year-old, had speech delays. Billy, also five, had cerebral palsy. Many of his IEP goals were directed at fine motor skills. These boys had observed but not actively participated in several previous projects, and they would be attending kindergarten the following fall. I wanted them involved more extensively in this last project of the year so that they could become more independent learners. Both Brandon and Billy had previously had difficulties working cooperatively with other children and staying with an activity for extended periods of time.

PHASE I: BEGINNING THE PROJECT

I selected birds as the topic for this project because they could be observed and studied in a variety of settings that were easily accessible to us. Birds were all around us—in the classroom, on the playground, at a nearby park, and in the neighborhood around the school. The children were very interested in this topic from the beginning.

We introduced the topic by taking a walk and observing signs of spring in the quad area of nearby Eureka College. While on the walk, we observed a large brown bird making a nest. The children immediately began guessing what kind of bird we had observed, and during snack time, they discussed how they could get closer to it (PS5: *Increase opportunities for collaborative problem solving*). That very day, during small-group time, I asked what they already knew about birds, and I wrote down their thoughts in the form of a list (PS1: *Encourage small-group discussion*; PS2: *Promote increased vocabulary*).

I wanted to build their background knowledge on birds, so the next day I brought in informational books and some photos of birds of prey that I found in a magazine at the library (PS2: *Promote increased vocabulary*). The children and I also invited the biology teacher from the high school to accompany us on our next walk to the campus. We asked her if she would help us to identify the big brown bird, and she did. It was a brown eagle! She helped the children find answers to their questions in reference books that she brought along with her, and she also shared diagrams and posters of birds with us. The children used this information to draw birds (see Figure 5.7; PS2: *Promote increased vocabulary*; PS3: *Support investigation*; PS4: *Support representing information*).

Several families had pet birds and brought them into the classroom for observation and discussion. This was very helpful, since they were usually willing to leave the birds in the classroom all day. It gave us time to observe, draw, and talk about the birds (see Figure 5.8; PS1: *Encourage small-group discussion*; PS3: *Support investigation*; PS4: *Support representing information*). This was the fifth or sixth project for some of these parents. They had a fairly good understanding of how the project approach worked and realized the value of extended time for study. In addition to bringing pet birds in to visit, many parents also volunteered to help with project

Figure 5.7 Diagram of a bird donated by a biology teacher and child's diagram of the bird.

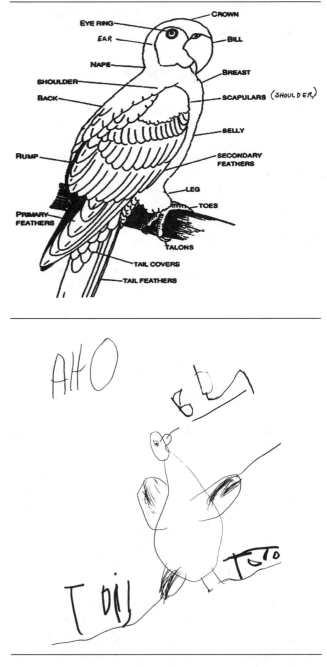

Figure 5.8 Children observe and draw a pet bird belonging to a student's family.

activities in the classroom or accompany us on our walks to the campus quad. Other project activities that families were able to assist with included building birdhouses and bird feeders.

As the children listened to the guest expert and observed the pet birds, I observed the children. I could see that they were becoming interested in both the environments for pet birds and the bird feeders. During small-group time, the children generated the following questions for investigation:

How do birds fly?
Why do they like trees?
Where are their noses?
Where are their feet?
Where are their ears?
What do birds eat?
What are their wings made of?
Do they have tails?
How do they talk?
How do they sing?
How come they have so many colors?
How do birds sleep? (PS1: *Encourage small-group discussion*; PS3: *Support investigation*)

PHASE II: INVESTIGATION

The children learned about birds and their environments by studying and representing them (PS4: *Support representing information*). Several of the children became engaged in constructing bird feeders and birdhouses, including Brandon (PS4: *Increase opportunities for collaborative problem solving*). As a reference for their constructions, the children used informational books and photographs taken during visits to the classroom by guest experts and pets. Such records of the children's experiences are often very valuable resources because they help children remember what they have previously learned. Brandon and Billy became particularly interested in painting a large mural of the brown eagle's environment, which we had observed on our walks, and they made use of these reference materials (see Figure 5.9; PS3: *Support purposeful writing and art*).

During Phase II we invited a bird expert from Wildlife Prairie Park to visit and answer the children's questions (PS3: *Support investigation*). The expert brought several live birds of prey with her, including an eagle. The children observed the birds' flight patterns, helped measure their wing spans, and got close enough to see the birds' talons and beaks. After this visit, three of the boys decided to construct a brown eagle (see Figure 5.10). I was pleased that Brandon and Billy were part of this group. The construction took almost two weeks; they used scrap materials and then wrote a descriptive story about the bird's characteristics (PS4: *Support representing information*; PS5: *Increase opportunities for collaborative problem solving*; PS6: *Support purposeful writing and art*; PS7: *Provide for gross motor skill development*).

The children were absorbed and engrossed in their work. As they progressed through each step of their investigation, they shared their discoveries and achievements with the class and invited people to visit and see and hear about the results of their investigation (PS1: *Encourage small-group discussion*; PS4: *Support representing information*). They *explained* what happened in the process of construction. In fact, the children were so engaged in building their eagle that they sometimes became quite emotional while reaching a consensus about what to do or how to do it. For example, I heard one boy say, "It's got to have hanging down feathers, Spencer, 'cause they really do have 'em!" (PS1: *Encourage small-group discussion*).

It is always exciting to see the problem solving that takes place during project work. For example, Brandon was very determined to put a brain into the head of the brown eagle. He tried several different methods before he found one that satisfied him. He discussed and brainstormed with the other children. First he tried inserting

Figure 5.9 Mural of the brown eagle's environment.

they dug an indentation in the belly of their eagle and embedded the claws into it (PS6: *Support purposeful writing and art*; PS7: *Provide for gross motor skill development*).

The children were also motivated to learn and use important knowledge, skills, and dispositions related to literacy during the Bird Project. We had a bird word wall that the children used as a reference. Because they made frequent use of the word wall, the children began to recognize many bird-related words in the books and stories I read with them (PS2: *Promote increased vocabulary*).

I was pleased to see Billy involved in this aspect of the project. As discussed above, Billy often avoided fine motor activities, so several of his IEP goals were directed toward these kinds of activities. This interest in birds led him to participate in more activities involving fine motor skills. Billy tried drawing and labeling for the first time; for example, he drew a representation of a bird's anatomy, drew lines that could be used to label the anatomy, and contributed several entries to the word wall (PS2: *Promote increased vocabulary*; PS6: *Support purposeful writing and art*). I observed Billy achieve many of his IEP goals and saw documentation of many of the items on the Work Sampling Checklist as Billy took part in the investigation. The Bird Project

Figure 5.10 The children used reference materials to construct the brown eagle.

a picture of a brain that he had sketched. Then he made a brain out of Play-Doh but that method did not satisfy him either. His solution was to wad up gray tissue paper until he thought it looked like a brain (PS4: *Support representing information*; PS5: *Increase opportunities for collaborative problem solving*). He said the brain was necessary "because eagles are pretty smart birds, Mrs. Scranton." His comment reflected a growing disposition to respect birds.

As they studied and constructed the eagle, the boys learned more about them. For example, they learned that an eagle brings its talons in toward its tummy during flight and then brings them down at the last minute before landing, just like an airplane lowering its wheels (PS2: *Promote increased vocabulary*). The boys represented this learning in their construction. They used craft sticks and slinky coils to create claws, and then motivated him to participate in many fine motor activities, and I observed tremendous improvement in his writing skills (see Figure 5.11). In fact, Billy's writing improved so much that another child, Spencer, made a comment during word wall work about his writing: "Billy is a writer like me, huh, Mrs. Scranton?"

The project also helped some of the children learn to work together. For example, the construction of a birdhouse was begun in response to the children's interest in wild bird environments. Brandon's IEP goals were directed toward his behavior disorder. He sometimes had difficulty using appropriate behaviors, but he desperately wanted to work on the construction of a birdhouse. He loved tools, and this provided a

Figure 5.11 Billy wrote *birdhouse* and *feathers* for the word wall.

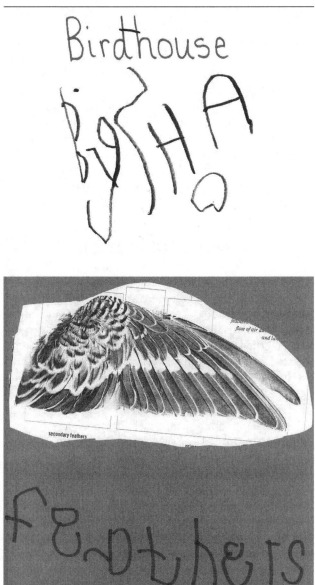

Figure 5.12 Children work together to hammer a birdhouse.

strong motivation to meet the challenge of working cooperatively and sharing tools with two other children (see Figure 5.12; PS5: *Increase opportunities for collaborative problem solving*). His leadership in the construction of the eagle also earned him the genuine admiration of other children in the class. I overheard several children say things like, "Wow, Brandon! That's a cool eagle!" Brandon just beamed; he was so proud of his accomplishment.

Additional questions about birds were generated throughout the Bird Project, especially after the expert from Wildlife Prairie Park brought the actual birds of prey to our classroom. The group of boys who constructed the eagle were especially interested in what foods these birds eat and how they hunt for their food. Two of the questions they asked were, "How do they chew their food?" and "Is it dead when they eat it?" The children also remained curious about other kinds of birds in Eureka. Throughout the project, we repeatedly visited the campus quad at Eureka College. This was especially helpful because we could observe several species at the same time and take good digital photos (PS3: *Support investigation*).

The children produced many products during the Bird Project: Time 1/Time 2 sketches (see Figure 5.13), a mural, birdhouses and bird feeders, bird diagrams, the bird word wall, and the brown eagle construction (PS4: *Support representing information*). The brown eagle construction was particularly special to me, however, because two of my students with special needs were involved. It was so wonderful to see them absorbed in

Figure 5.13 Time 1 and Time 2 drawings of a lovebird, made four days apart. Notice the increased detail and proportion.

a topic, working with others, and, most importantly, taking pride in everything they had learned.

PHASE III: CONCLUDING THE PROJECT

Children were very involved in documenting this project (PS4: *Support representing information*). They wrote descriptive stories about their work that reflected what they had learned about the topic (PS2: *Promote increased vocabulary*; PS6: *Support purposeful writing and art*). The story dictated by Brandon about the brown eagle demonstrated how much the boys had learned about the characteristics of brown eagles:

> We built a eagle. A.J. made his tail. It has feathers on it. Spencer made the talons. Talons are for catching fish, but he is gonna' eat mice, too. He gots wings to help him fly. Our eagle likes to live in high, high trees by high, high mountains. I maded his head and put in gray stuff for his brain. This eagle's got to have a brain 'cause he's a very smart bird.

As the project came to a close, their work was displayed. The mural was hung in the classroom, and the descriptive story about the brown eagle was placed near the constructed eagle. The bird feeders were filled with bird food and installed on the campus quad. The birdhouse was suspended from a tree across the street from our classroom so that we could observe the birds as they nested in it, and the completed brown eagle construction was hung from the classroom ceiling so that it looked as if it were flying. The work produced by the children revealed that they had learned a great deal. As a culminating event, the children gave tours of their work to children from two other classrooms. The children also made a book to share with their parents, and they sent the "bird lady" a diary that described the efforts of the group that constructed the eagle (PS4: *Support representing information*; PS6: *Support purposeful writing and art*).

TEACHER REFLECTIONS

The children learned so much during this project! They learned about the environment in Eureka and why so many different species of birds are found there in the old trees; about bird anatomy, habits, and the role that birds play in our ecosystem; and to use found materials to create constructions. However, I believe the greatest gains were made in their observational skills. It seemed to me that for the first time this group of children really *watched* and *listened* to what was around them, which was very exciting for me.

Another strength of this particular project was the way it involved families. They became more aware of our word wall, for example. The wall was truly impressive by the end of the Bird Project. It was very full and illustrated how many new words were learned during the project. Families also were impressed with the level of interest that the children maintained to complete a large construction like the brown eagle.

What was perhaps most meaningful to me in this project was the growth I saw in my students with special needs. There was a dramatic turnaround in Brandon's behavior and in his ability to work and play with other children. I was similarly pleased with Billy's sudden interest and increased skill in writing and drawing.

Through this project I learned that even the child who faces the most difficult challenges is able to succeed in project work. Absorption and intense work during a project allows hidden strengths to shine through.

REFERENCES

Accommodating all children in the early childhood classroom. (1999). Retrieved January 2001 from University of Kansas Web site: http://www.circleofinclusion.org/

Bredekamp, S., & Copple, C. (1997). *Developmentally appropriate practice in early childhood programs* (Rev. ed.). Washington, DC: National Association for the Education of Young Children.

Department of Education, U.S. (2000). *Twenty-second annual report to Congress on the implementation of the Individuals with Disabilities Education Act.* Washington, DC: U.S. Department of Education.

Edmiaston, R. (1998). Projects in inclusive early childhood classrooms. In J. H. Helm (Ed.), *The project approach catalog 2 by the project approach study group* (sec. 1, pp. 23–26). Champaign, IL: ERIC Clearinghouse on Elementary and Early Childhood Education.

Farran, D. (2000). Another decade of intervention. In J. Shonkoff & S. Meisels (Eds.), *Handbooks of early childhood intervention* (2nd ed.) (pp. 510–548). Cambridge, UK: Cambridge University Press.

Klein, N., & Gilkerson, L. (2000). Personnel preparation for early childhood intervention programs. In J. Shonkoff & S. Meisels (Eds.), *Handbooks of early childhood intervention* (2nd ed.) (pp. 454–483). Cambridge, UK: Cambridge University Press.

Sandall, S., McLean, M., & Smith, B. (2000). *DEC recommended practices in early intervention/early childhood special education.* Denver, CO: Council for Exceptional Children, Division for Early Childhood.

Shonkoff, J., & Meisels, S. (Eds.). (2000). *Handbook of early childhood intervention.* Cambridge, UK: Cambridge University Press.

Villa, R. A., Klift, E. V. D., Udis, J., Thousand, J. S., Nevin, A. I., Kune, N., & Chapple, J. W. (1995). Questions, concerns, beliefs, and practical advice about inclusive environments. In R. A. Villa & J. S. Thousand (Eds.), *Creating an inclusive school* (pp. 136–61). Alexandria, VA: Association for Supervision and Curriculum Development.

Wolery, M., & Wilburs, J. S. (1994). Introduction to the inclusion of young children with special needs in early childhood programs. In M. Wolery & J. S. Wilbers (Eds.), *Including children with special needs in early childhood programs* (pp. 1–22). Washington, DC: National Association for the Education of Young Children.

Wolery, R. A., & Odom, S. L. (2000). *An administrator's guide to preschool inclusion.* Chapel Hill: University of North Carolina, Frank Porter Graham Child Development Center, Early Childhood Research Institute on Inclusion.

CHAPTER 6

Supporting Second-Language Learners

Contributors: Judy Harris Helm and Rebecca A. Wilson

DEFINING THE CHALLENGE
Judy Harris Helm and Rebecca A. Wilson

In classrooms all across the United States there are second-language learners. These children may be in regular classrooms, transitional bilingual programs, or pull-out English as a second language (ESL) programs for children acquiring English. The number of children learning a second language has grown significantly over the last decade. According to the National Clearinghouse on Bilingual Education (Antunez & Zelasko, August 2001), instructional programs for English-language learners (ELL) are grouped under two main categories based on the language(s) used to provide instruction. In bilingual education, content instruction is provided through both English and the students' native language while the students develop English proficiency. In ESL programs, all instruction is provided in English only. Most bilingual education programs in the United States include an ESL component. How these bilingual and ESL programs are implemented varies widely. Dual-language programs provide instruction in both languages for all children in the class. ESL programs may provide direct instruction in English as part of the normal classroom curriculum or provide support to children in separate, English-only classrooms. Typically, schools use a combination of instructional models that include some elements of bilingual education and ESL. Some children in the class may be native English speakers who are learning a second language. In early childhood education, these second-language learners are often in some type of bilingual program in which they learn the second language as they develop reading and writing skills in English.

There is considerable confusion and debate about how young children learn a second language. Although many teachers believe that learning a second language is easy for children, this is probably not true. Young children do not have access to the memory techniques and other strategies that more experienced learners can use in acquiring vocabulary and learning the grammatical rules of the language (McLaughlin, 1992).

Many educators today have children in their classrooms who are learning a second language, yet few teachers have been trained in how to foster second-language development or know about the process of second-language learning. Children who are learning English as a second language face many more hurdles in schools where English is the only language used for instruction. These children are also more likely to have discipline problems and to drop out of school before their education is completed.

Bilingualism, however, also brings advantages to children. Being bilingual has definite economic advantages and increases career opportunities (McLaughlin, 1995). For this to happen, however, it is important that the home language be preserved and strengthened if children are instructed entirely in English. Children in classrooms where English is the dominant language also often experience cultural conflict because the routines of communication in the classroom may not match the ways they are accustomed to learning. Some communication patterns that are related to culture include being silent, not participating in classroom activities or calling attention to oneself, expressing joy or emotions in different ways, and the pacing of activities. An important aspect of culture that can affect teaching and learning involves how teachers use language during instruction: "For example, if the home culture values strict authority of adults over children and if children are only supposed to speak when spoken to, then these same students may be reluctant to volunteer an answer in class" (Peregoy & Boyle, 1993, p. 10). The warmth of the classroom and how comfortable a child feels with the teacher also influence language acquisition.

Children vary greatly in their motivation to learn a new language. It is important that language be meaningful. In addition to learning a second language, children with home languages other than English may have immigrant parents with low literacy skills. Reading and writing, even in the first language, may not be part of the child's home culture. This can impact the child's motivation to become literate in either language and to be part of a school community that emphasizes literacy.

Especially challenging for teachers in bilingual or ESL programs is the task of obtaining relevant and meaningful literacy materials. Many teachers find it necessary to spend a significant amount of time making books, signs, and other materials that can be used for meaningful literacy instruction for second-language learners.

PRACTICAL STRATEGIES
Rebecca A. Wilson

I have found that the project approach works very well for second-language learners. In my dual-language kindergarten classroom at West Liberty Elementary School in Iowa, all of the students are learning a second language. Spanish speakers are learning English, and English speakers are learning Spanish. A dual-language, bilingual classroom is one of the many ways to meet the needs of second-language learners.

The project approach enables me to connect academic content to children's experiences and to integrate curriculum goals in meaningful ways. As Eugene Garcia wrote:

> The more linguistically and culturally diverse the children, the more closely teachers must relate academic content to a child's own environment and experience.
> The more diverse the children, the more integrated the curriculum should be. . . .
> The more diverse the children, the greater the need for active rather than passive endeavors. . . .
> The more diverse the children, the more important it is to offer them opportunities to apply what they are learning in a meaningful context (quoted in Ovando & Collier, 1998, p. 86).

Several recommendations for teaching second-language learners can be integrated easily into project work. Lily

Wong Fillmore has studied the processes by which children acquire English as a second language under various conditions in public schools. She strongly emphasizes the importance of children maintaining their primary language while acquiring a second language. The language-rich environment of projects provides many opportunities for this to happen. Wong Fillmore (1985) proposed a model for teaching second-language learners that is applicable to many types of classrooms and recommends that teachers adopt the following strategies:

- Use demonstrations
- Model and role-play
- Provide new information in the context of known information
- Repeat words and sentence patterns
- Tailor questions for different levels of language competence and participation

Below I will explain how each of these recommendations can be incorporated into project work, based on my experiences of using the project approach in my dual-language kindergarten classroom. I will also show how a teacher can maximize the project experience to benefit second-language learners.

In addition to Wong Fillmore's (1985) recommendations, I would like to add two other important strategies for teaching second-language learners: value native language and encourage parent involvement. A recent case study of eight high-performance Hispanic schools in Texas concluded that they were successful for three main reasons:

1. They collaborated with community groups and businesses.
2. They established strong working relationships with parents and the community at large.
3. As centers of learning for the local community, they integrated local cultural values into the school culture. (Reyes & Halcon, 2000)

Although many examples in this chapter focus on dual-language classrooms, these strategies can be used in any classroom with one or more second-language learners.

Practical Strategy 1:
Use Demonstrations

Second-language learners can process a concept much better if information is presented to them visually rather than solely through language. Learning through

Figure 6.1 Mimi studies the teeth model.

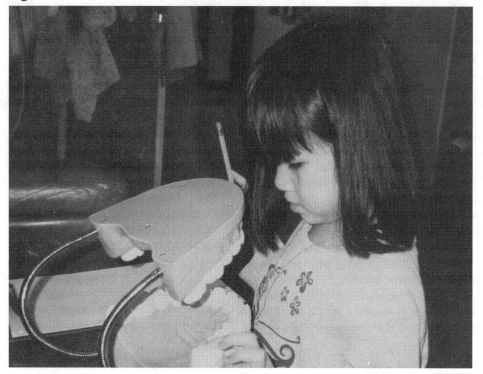

real life situations is very effective for second-language learners. Research shows that the quality of exposure to the second language, not just the quantity, is important for effective learning. Second-language input must be comprehensible in order to promote second-language acquisition (Krashen, 1996). What better way to make a concept comprehensible than to demonstrate it?

Teachers can develop demonstrations about the project topic; many times, the experts and field-site hosts can provide demonstration ideas. Teachers can encourage the children to remember the demonstration by bringing artifacts into the classroom as a follow-up. In Figure 6.1, Mimi, a native speaker of Chinese learning to speak English, manipulates and studies an artifact brought back to her preschool from a site visit. The artifact enables Mimi to participate in investigation of the project topic, teeth, without having to rely only on verbal information. Mimi's growth in knowledge and understanding can be seen by comparing her Time 1 and Time 2 drawings of teeth (Figure 6.2). Mimi also was motivated to copy an English word onto her paper.

During projects, I arrange to have demonstrations related to aspects of the topic that are of high interest to the children. If the demonstration is based on second-language learners' interests, they are more likely to focus on the demonstration, even in their second language. If the teachers do not speak the native language of the second-language learners in the class, they can look for nonverbal clues indicating that the child is interested. For example, when a child moves closer while a teacher reads a story and shows pictures about a particular subject, or if a child brings in an object, such as a bird's nest, that was found on the playground and keeps pointing to it, the child is demonstrating interest. A teacher guiding a project can observe children's play or discussions to see what topic might make a good focus of a demonstration. The Restaurant Project originated from a group of children repeatedly playing "restaurant" in our dramatic play area. They pretended to be customers and waiters. Consequently, on our field-site visit I arranged for an employee of the restaurant to demonstrate how to take an order in Spanish. The Spanish-speaking employee helped Joel and Jorge ask what another student, Ariel, wanted to eat and helped them write it down. This helped the English-speaking students in my room understand *¿Qué quieren comer?* (What do you want to eat?) If I taught those words in isolation in the classroom, the children might have difficulty understanding what they meant, but seeing the demonstration enabled them to understand almost immediately.

Demonstration worked equally well with Spanish speakers in my class practicing their English. During a field visit in the Combine Project, a farmer demonstrated how he harvested soybeans by operating his combine where we all could see it. He cut a path down the middle of the field to show how the soybeans were disappearing. This helped all children in my class bet-

Figure 6.2 Mimi's first drawing of teeth is simple. In her second drawing, she includes the parts of a tooth and also copies the word *Teeth* in English.

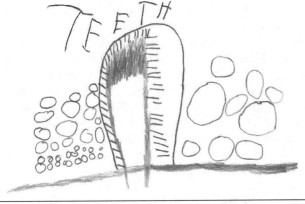

ter understand the concept of *harvest*. It certainly helped my Spanish-speaking children learn the words *combine* and *soybeans*. Talking about the harvest process, even using a visual aid such as photos in a nonfiction book, would not have created the depth of understanding that my students had after witnessing the combine in action. Even when there is only one child in the class who does not speak the language of instruction, that child better understands the English words by seeing the demonstration.

For maximum benefit, the demonstrations can be experienced again in the classroom by videotaping the event and/or by bringing in a variety of tools used during the demonstration. As another demonstration during the Combine Project, the bolts on the wheel of a tractor were removed. This particular demonstration was selected because the children were very interested in the wheels on the combines and tractors. Afterwards, the local tractor dealership loaned our class the air wrench and bolts. The children were able to examine the air wrench closely and to see how the bolts fit into the end of it. It was a language-rich part of the children's investigation and promoted extensive conversation between English and Spanish speakers.

Practical Strategy 2: Incorporate Modeling and Role-Play

Modeling and role-play are natural ways for second-language learners to practice language, and role-play is almost inevitable in project work. Children become so involved in investigating a particular project that their free time is often spent acting out scenarios about the topic. Creating dramatic play environments encourages role-play and the use of language related to the topic, especially if children are involved in creating the environment or play structure (Helm & Katz, 2001).

Teachers of second-language learners will find it helpful to provide plenty of time for role-play during a project. More hesitant students will be encouraged to become involved through a teacher's modeling of role-play. Role-play also emerges in the preparation for field-site visits or expert visitors. Teachers and children can role-play asking the experts questions so that the children feel comfortable on the day of a field-site or expert visit. In our classroom, role-playing questions in advance of visits helped many of my students to independently ask questions in their second language.

Role-play provides children with the opportunity to meaningfully interact with their second language. During the Fire Station Project, children chose to create a fire truck, complete with hoses, in the classroom. I noticed high levels of play from my students. One day during center time, a mixed group of English and Spanish speakers were role-playing about putting out fires. Second-language communication occurred frequently. A native English-speaking child was on the student-made computer and radio, calling out the name of the street with the fire to two children dressed up as firefighters, one native English speaker and one native Spanish speaker. As they fought the fire with their hoses, also created by students, I heard them communicating to each other, "Bring the hose over here," and "The fire's getting bigger!" As the Spanish-speaking "firefighter" reported in English that the fire was getting bigger, the child on the radio said that it had moved, "All the way up to 15th Street now!" A fourth and fifth child, one native Spanish speaker and one native English speaker, alternated between driving the fire truck and making the fire on a nearby chalkboard "grow" by adding more lines and scribbles. This native Spanish-speaking child demonstrated growth in receptive language as he interpreted the English words *bigger* and *grow* by making more lines on the chalkboard as the firefighters reported the status of the fire. When the fire was out at last, the two firefighters reported it to the two drivers, who then erased it from the chalkboard.

Role-play can be observed in both ESL and bilingual classrooms during project work. In another kindergarten classroom in our building there is a child whose native language is Laotian. Center time is beneficial for him because he can participate in dramatic play. He has the chance to try out words he has heard in the classroom in the context of role-play.

I can honestly say that I have never seen such involved role-play in my kindergarten classroom as I do when we are in the middle of a project. The children are so engaged that they hardly notice me observing their play. This high level of play (i.e., more complex roles, language consistent with the role, more playmates interacting) stems from the length of project work and the children's interest, and I do not believe it would occur in a shorter, teacher-directed unit. The high level of play that occurs in projects aids second-language learners in their understanding and use of language in a meaningful manner. At the same time, because of the spontaneous nature of play, children often continue to use their native language, thereby encouraging language development in their primary language. Language-rich play can help the child achieve additive bilingualism as opposed to subtractive bilingualism.

Practical Strategy 3:
Introduce New Information in the Context of Known Information

Providing new information in the context of known information is easily incorporated into the project approach. Graphic organizers, a frequently used strategy for ESL teachers, are used in almost all projects. These include planning webs, question lists, word walls, project books and dictionaries, all of which help second-language learners, as well as emergent readers, organize and process information.

When first beginning a project, I web with my students to record what they already know about the topic. I accept children's answers in whatever language they are offered, but I say them back and record them on the web in the language we are currently speaking in the classroom. This helps second-language learners feel comfortable and capable of contributing to the discussion, but it also helps them develop their second language by hearing the word said back to them and watching it being written on the web. In addition, this process develops first-language learning and promotes true bilingualism.

When teachers use webs in project work, they often record a picture next to the word so that students can understand what is being discussed. For example, during the Fire Station Project our class was making a web, and the language used in the classroom at that time of the day was Spanish. A Spanish speaker suggested that I write *camión* (fire truck) on the web. A few days later we were speaking in Spanish again, and the children

were making a book of things they had seen at the fire station. Drake, a native English speaker, asked me, "How do you say truck again in Spanish?" I was able to point to our web and said the first letter sound, and he was able to remember that the word was *camión*. The web validates all children's knowledge and gives them a chance to build on the information they already know. The students refer back to the web often when they are working independently on journals or want to write a particular word. If a teacher does not speak the language of the child, she or he can accept the child's contribution to the web by asking the second-language learner to draw an illustration on the web. This works well if other children are also drawing on the web.

In much the same way, second-language learners benefit when question lists are made and words recorded on a word wall. Since most of the children in my classroom are emergent readers, I am careful to also include a drawing so that they can understand the words. During a project on automotive service stations, a group of children spent several days working on project dictionaries or books using the words that interested them from the word wall. We worked on the dictionaries over a span of several days, both at times we were speaking Spanish and English. The children helped each other by pointing out words they knew in the different languages.

Practical Strategy 4:
Repeat Word and Sentence Patterns

Because the project approach focuses on a topic in depth for long periods of time, it is easy for teachers of second-language learners to support repetition of words and word patterns. It is important for second-language learners to have the chance to hear words several times and have many opportunities to repeat the words in meaningful situations. One of the biggest differences I notice between project work and other work is the rich vocabulary children use while involved in projects. At times the specific vocabulary being used by children is amazing considering they are only five years old. Halfway through the Combine Project, we visited a local tractor dealership to answer children's more detailed questions about tractors and combines. We walked into a large room where vehicles were being repaired, and one of my students immediately said, "Look, Mrs. Wilson, there's an auger!" In the Garden Project, children were referring to the "three tine cultivator," and during the Restaurant Project, children spoke extensively of the cash register, menus, and prices. During block play connected with the Fire Station Project, I overheard one of the children say, "Wait, I'm going to add one more vehicle."

The rich vocabulary in the children's project work supports second-language learners for two reasons. First, they hear the words referred to again and again as children become interested in certain parts of the project. For example, during the Restaurant Project, almost everyone in the class knew the word for *menu* in both Spanish and English. Second, during project work everyone is involved in learning new vocabulary. Children are talking about different words, asking questions about what words mean, and writing or drawing pictures of newly acquired words that interest them. Children learning a second language fit right in. Because everyone is engaged in learning new vocabulary, second-language learners are less likely to feel embarrassed or shy, even if the vocabulary words they are picking out of the project in their second language are simple and not necessarily specialized.

Practical Strategy 5:
Tailor Questions for Language Level

Wong Fillmore (1985) recommends that questions be tailored to different levels of language competence and participation. Questioning is one of the most important parts of project work. A quick way to tell how involved children truly are in a project is through a list of their questions. Teachers should encourage all children in the class to ask questions; some may require only a simple yes or no answer. For example, during the Garden Project, a native Spanish speaker felt comfortable asking an expert gardener visitor, "Do you have a hose?" She was able to understand his answer, "yes," and record it independently on her paper. During the Fire Station project, one native Spanish speaker asked the more complicated question, "How do you turn on the sirens?" Both types of questions are accepted and recorded. As with webbing in our dual-language classroom, I accept the language choice of the child, and repeat his or her question in the language our class is speaking at the moment. I also frequently draw something next to the question to remind second-language learners and emergent readers what the question says.

In a classroom where the teacher does not speak the same language as a second-language learner, he or she might take the child aside during center or work time to show him or her some pictures of the subject and ask the child to point to something interesting. For example, during the Combine Project, if I did not speak Spanish, I might work with my native Spanish speakers individually during center time and show them some photos of the combine. I would try to draw out of them what they wanted to know more about by asking simple questions and repeating them with gestures. For example, I might display several photos showing different aspects of the object we are studying. In a project on combines, I might display a photo of a combine wheel and the front, dashboard, and rear of the machine. With a wordless gesture, Gabriela might point to the wheels or the lights, leading me in the direction of her interests. Even if the teacher does not speak the child's language, during project work he or she can get an idea of what the child's area of questioning may be.

Because project work occurs over a long period of time, children have many opportunities to ask questions. The children's questions are often used as clues for teachers to know where to go next with the project. It enables them to reflect the interests of the children in their teaching, which is especially valuable for second-language learners. As pointed out earlier, a child is much more likely to listen to something in a second language if they are interested in the topic.

Practical Strategy 6:
Value Native Language

Research shows that valuing a child's native language will help pave the way to academic success in the future. Studies state that bilingual students of Hispanic/Latino heritage are better readers in English and have higher academic aspirations than Hispanic/Latino students that are monolingual in either Spanish or English. This suggests that students who have developed or valued their native language do better in school, both in Spanish and English, than those who leave their native language behind (Tse, 2001).

The project approach provides many opportunities for teachers to value the native language of second-language learners. When culturally relevant topics are chosen, second-language learners are validated. In examining a topic carefully before beginning a project, I consider if it is mentioned in the everyday play and conversations of second-language learners. It is important to have some of the projects during a school year focus on a topic that relates to the culture or home life of at least some of the second-language learners in the class. If possible, teachers can then choose a field-site visit where there may be native speakers of their home language.

Practical Strategy 7:
Involve Parents of Second-Language Learners in Project Work

An important benefit of using the project approach with children learning a second language is the increased level of parental involvement in classrooms. Although parental involvement is extremely important for all children, the promotion of strong home-school partnerships is especially beneficial for second-language learners (Goldenberg, 1993). Yet it can be challenging for teachers to communicate with parents. Espinosa (1995) points out that flyers or newsletters sent home may still be ineffective with Hispanic parents even when translated into Spanish, because many Spanish speakers prefer oral to written communication. The strategies Espinosa recommends to involve Hispanic parents in early childhood classrooms include taking a personal approach and engaging in nonjudgmental communication. She states that it may take "several personal meetings before parents gain trust to actively participate" (p. 3). Nonverbal communication that supports parents' strengths rather than focusing on what may be perceived failings is also extremely important.

The strategies suggested by Espinosa can be met by using the project approach, which provides parents with numerous opportunities to personally visit the classroom in addition to parent-teacher conferences. During projects, parents can come to informational nights and family nights celebrating culminating events, especially if those events are held at times when parents can attend. Parents can also help with field-site visits.

An additional way to involve parents is to choose culturally relevant topics and draw on and support the language-minority parents' strengths. Parents can benefit as well from experiences in a project that is rich with language. They can serve as expert consultants or contribute artifacts for the class to sketch. For example, in the Mexican Restaurant Project, parents could have shared their own stories about cooking or perform demonstrations with the children.

Many occasions, such as the parent informational night on projects and project family nights, encourage language-minority parents to feel at ease and network with other families. Another way to increase the comfort level of language-minority families while at school is to have the children show their parents around during the project night so families can celebrate their learning together. In our classroom, the day before a project family night, children practice pointing out their contributions to the project so that they can share them with their families.

Parents of second-language learners can also contribute to the project by providing needed materials from home and sharing home vocabulary for words related to the project. During a project on an automotive service station, the children decided they wanted a blue shirt for a mechanic to wear, which was contributed by parents. A Spanish-speaking father taught me the word for *hoist*, which I did not know and could not find in the Spanish-English dictionary.

If the teacher does not speak the language of the child, the school can usually find someone in the community to translate any written communications into the home language. Even if the bilingual community person or parent can only meet once with the teacher, the teacher can find out how to write the days of the week and the times in the home language as well as a few other key words, which will enable accurate communication about important classroom events. If this is not a possibility, newsletters or information about project nights can be communicated most effectively in English by reducing the message to only the most important information and using many illustrations. For example, a detailed invitation to parents might be changed to read "Project Night—Thursday, March 14th 6:00 p.m." with some clip art or a drawing of families entering the school. Another helpful communication method is to pin a reminder onto children's shirts when they go home on the afternoon of an evening project-related event.

Within my dual-language classroom, I noticed an increase in parental involvement since I have started using the project approach. One of the ways teachers can encourage involvement in projects is through a parent informational meeting at the beginning of the year. The meeting can be held in both English and the second language spoken in the classroom. I also have found it helpful to provide child care for the families to encourage everyone's attendance. During the meeting, I list possible ways for parents to be involved in our projects, including ways they can help at home and at school. As a result of the parent meeting during the 2000–2001 school year, two parents volunteered to help in our room on a weekly basis, and 12 out of 21 families attended a Project Family Night culminating a project during the fall. Twenty out of twenty-one families attended the Project Family Night in the spring.

Typically in our school, about 50% of parents attend events in the evening, and I had only nine families come to the regular Open House during that same 2000–2001 school year. Parents appear to make a greater effort to come to project-related events, and parent participation in project work continues to be high for my classroom.

CONCLUSION

Project work is effective in meeting the needs of second-language learners and it provides the kind of experiences that are consistent with research findings on language-minority education.

Research examining language minority student performance in bilingual, ESL, and grade-level classes taught through collaborative discovery learning using meaningful, cognitively complex, interdisciplinary content has found that active learning accelerates language minority students' academic growth (Ovando & Collier, 1998, p. 65).

In summary, there are ample opportunities in project work to apply these recommended and practical second-language learning strategies:

1. Use demonstrations
2. Incorporate modeling and role-play
3. Introduce new information in the context of known information
4. Repeat word and sentence patterns
5. Tailor questions for language level
6. Value native language
7. Involve parents of second-language learners in project work

Project work offers many opportunities for second-language learners to be involved in the classroom. Very few adjustments need to be made in the project approach; teachers simply need to be aware of strategies already in place and adapt them. As shown in the following description of the Mexican Restaurant Project, project work has made a great difference in the education of second-language learners in my bilingual classroom; the same approach used in this project can be applied in many different programs, such as dual language, transitional bilingual, resource bilingual, and ESL.

THE MEXICAN RESTAURANT PROJECT
Rebecca A. Wilson

The Mexican Restaurant Project took place at West Elementary, part of West Liberty Community Schools in West Liberty, Iowa. Although this is a rural area, it has many of the characteristics usually associated with urban areas. Thirty-eight percent of the children in the school are from low-income families, and 51% are Latino. Parents have an option of sending their children to an English-only kindergarten classroom or to the dual-language kindergarten classroom where this project took place. The project lasted from late January until early March 2001. Teresa Salazar and Berta Esquivel, classroom paraprofessionals, assisted me with project activities.

PHASE I: BEGINNING THE PROJECT

In January, I noticed that many of the children were playing restaurant in the dramatic play center of our classroom. I decided to do a brief unit on food to encourage this play. When the restaurant play persisted, I decided that a project on restaurants might be successful (PS2: *Incorporate modeling and role-play*). We began by making a web of what the children already knew about restaurants. All of them had been to a restaurant before, and I provided literature in both English and Spanish about restaurants and food. The children eagerly generated a list of questions:

How do you make tacos?
How long does it take to make the food?
How do you make the food?
How do you make the tortillas?
How do you make the menus?
How many people work there?
How much does the food cost?
How much do the tortas cost?
How do people pay for the food?
How much do avocados cost?
Where do you get "chile" from?
How do you make the cold ice cream?

The children's questions helped focus the learning experiences that I planned. For example, I used their questions to organize them into groups for the field-site visit (PS5: *Tailor questions*).

PHASE II: INVESTIGATION

Phase II began with a visit to La Mexicana Restaurant. I selected La Mexicana because it was popular with both Spanish- and English-speaking families in the class. The restaurant was owned by the Elizondo family and run by the grown children and parents. They were willing to help with the project, even though they had no previous connection with my classroom. Jose, the adult son of the owner, gave us a tour of the restaurant and answered the questions the children had generated prior to our visit. Jose also helped Jorge and Joel take another student's order during the tour (see Figure 6.3; PS1: *Use demonstrations*).

In the seating area of the restaurant, the children did observational drawing; however, they were most interested in counting and copying. They counted the number of legs on the tables, the number of tables and chairs in the room, and the number of utensils on the tables. Some of them spent a long time copying words from the menu (PS4: *Repeat word and sentence patterns*). They wanted to be sure that they had enough information to make their own restaurant in the classroom (PS2: *Incorporate modeling and role-play*). While involved in these activities, they asked Jose these questions:

How do you make the menus?
¿Cuántas personas trabajan allí?
How many people work there? (PS5: *Tailor questions*)

Figure 6.3 Mr. Elizondo, the owner of La Mexicana, teaches Jorge how to take orders.

Mrs. Elizondo, the wife of Mr. Elizondo, Sr., was the cook at La Mexicana. She showed the children the kitchen, where they saw the food and plates and the procedure for taking orders with order papers (PS1: *Use demonstrations*). The children drew the stove, silverware and utensils, labels, recipes, and pots and pans (PS3: *Introduce information in context*). While in the kitchen, they asked the following questions:

How do you make tacos?
How long does it take to make the food?
Where do you keep your baker clothes?
Do you have special clothes for cooking?
¿Cómo hacen los tacos?
How do you make the food?
How do you make the tortillas? (PS5: *Tailor questions*)

Mr. Elizondo, the owner, showed the children the cash register, the method for ringing up a customer's bill, and where he placed the money (PS1: *Use demonstrations*). In this area of the restaurant, the children sketched in great detail the cash register, including the numbers on the cash register buttons. They also drew the phone that was near the cash register and the order pads (PS3: *Introduce information in context*). The children asked Mr. Elizondo the following questions:

How much does the food cost?
¿Cuántos cuestan las tortas?
¿Cómo paga la gente para la comida? (PS: *Tailor questions*)

The children did observational drawings of many of the things they saw at the restaurant (see Figure 6.4). The soda machine in the kitchen seemed to fascinate the children the most (see Figure 6.5). Jose demonstrated how to make the soda come out, and he talked to the children about the signs at the top of the machine, which indicated the choices to the customer (PS1: *Use demonstrations*).

Figure 6.4 Bianca collects data on the tables during the field trip. She represented the table and then wrote *12* to show how many tables were in the restaurant.

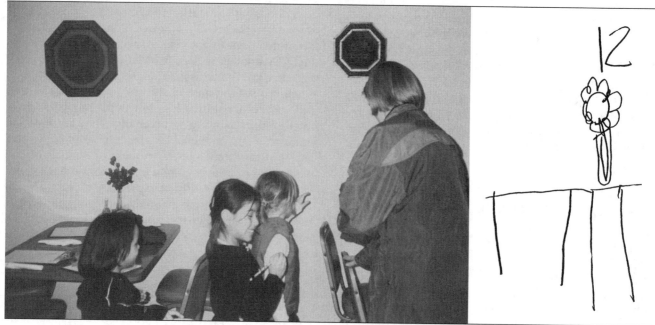

Figure 6.5 The children found the soda machine particularly interesting, and several children made observational drawings.

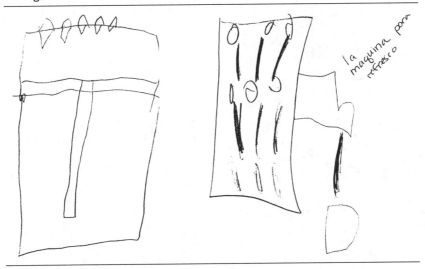

The front section of La Mexicana was a grocery store. Several of the children copied the print they observed on the shelved food items in the store (PS4: *Repeat word and sentence patterns*). They also did observational drawings of the shelves and counted the number of shelves; counted some of the food items and looked at their prices; and observed the way the food was organized by category (see Figure 6.6; PS3: *Introduce information in context*). Questions asked in this area of the store included

¿Cuántos cuestan los aguacates? (Anahi)
Where do you get "chile" from? (Morgan)
¿Cómo hacen las paletas frías? (PS5: *Tailor questions*)

The children were fascinated with what they were doing. At the field-site visit, they remained focused on their drawings and questions for half an hour, and did not want to return to school when the bus came to pick us up. They were also extremely pleased with the developed photos of the visit, and they enjoyed describing

Figure 6.6 The children make observational sketches of the canned goods in the grocery store at La Mexicana.

Figure 6.7 Morgan included her drawing of the shelves in her thank you note to Mr. Jose Elizondo.

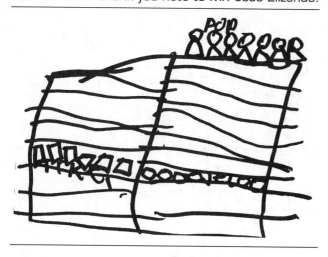

what they were doing in them (PS1: *Use demonstrations*). For example, Daniel said, "I was writing the letters on the bottles of pop." Ariel said, "He's ordering. You look at the words to order the food." Jessica said, "I'm in the store of La Mexicana reading the names of things."

The students began to bring in materials from home. One girl brought in pictures of food that she had cut out of magazines at home. That day, she and a friend chose to spend the entire 50 minutes of center time labeling all of the foods so that they could use them in the class's restaurant. One girl labeled the foods in English, and the other labeled them in Spanish (PS4: *Repeat word and sentence patterns*; PS6: *Value native language*).

The children thought quite a bit about what they had seen at La Mexicana, and this helped them decide what to build in their own restaurant (PS2: *Incorporate modeling and role-play*). A list was made of what was needed for the class restaurant, and children signed up for construction teams. As the children began to create their own restaurant, they produced many pictures, constructions, and signs (see Figures 6.7 and 6.8). For several days they made signs for the restaurant and hung them above the dramatic play center and in the hallway next to the door to our classroom. They also made menus, a soda machine, a cash register, and grocery store shelves. After the children had made a list of what to put in their restaurant, I provided the teams with several different sized boxes. The styrofoam pieces were left in the boxes, in case they wanted to use them as well. In addition to the boxes, there was always a wide variety of materials in the art and writing centers that the children could use, such as paper, collage materials, and several types of writing utensils.

The children were very interested in making the menus. They studied the menus they had borrowed from La Mexicana for a long time and then began to make their own (see Figure 6.9; PS4: *Repeat word and sentence patterns*; PS6: *Value native language*). Kathy became the menu "expert" and started making several menus (see Figures 6.10 and 6.11). Each menu contained exactly the same food for sale at exactly the same prices. Several other children became interested in the process, and they also began to make menus. Making the menus provided the children with significant practice in writing letters and numerals (see Figure 6.12; PS4: *Repeat word and sentence patterns*). The children understood the concept that the customer must read the words on a menu to see what food the restaurant can make. They understood that the menu helps the customer decide what to order. Ordering food from the menu was an ongoing part of the dramatic play in the class restaurant (PS2: *Incorporate modeling and role-play*). Through this dramatic play, the children learned the power of using written words to record what people had ordered. For example, at La Mexicana, when Jose helped two

Figure 6.8 McKayla drew the store and the shelves from memory.

Figure 6.9 McKayla uses the real menu from La Mexicana as a reference for her own writing.

Figure 6.10 The cover of the menu Kathy made.

Figure 6.11 The inside of Kathy's menu reveals her use of inventive spelling and understanding of how to represent money.

members of our class take an order from two other children, one child asked for Sprite. Back in our classroom, these two children figured out how to represent *Sprite* on the order paper with the letter *S*.

The construction of the grocery store shelves provided a helpful experience in problem solving for the children. It was an opportunity to think "outside the box" to find a solution. First, they decided to use styrofoam to make the shelves (see Figure 6.13). They were planning to mount the shelves inside a tall box that was open on one side, but they discovered that they had cut the pieces of styrofoam too short. They tried many methods to get the shelves to stay in place, including tape and pushpins, but neither worked. Then they tried gluing the shelves. The children held the shelves in place while the glue dried, but despite their patience, the shelves fell when they released them. Finally, after several days of trial and error, they discovered that if they cut a shelf just the same size as the opening, it would stay in place on its own (see Figure 6.14). I was very impressed with how supportive the children were of one another when faced with the problem of the collapsing shelves, and how *all* members of the team were involved on different levels. For example, Paquito, a child with a severe language delay, contributed to the team's efforts by frequently announcing when the

Figure 6.12 Irving watches as children copy words off of the soda machine construction onto their menu.

shelves fell and helping to pick them up. He also tried to hold the shelves for the other children while the glue was drying. Paquito's participation provided a great example of how project work encourages all children to be involved and supportive of each other.

Many of the children's questions at the field site involved money and the exchange of money. Some of the children were curious about where the money was kept. This group of children studied the cash register at La Mexicana, so it seemed natural that they would want to work together to create the cash register for the class restaurant (PS1: *Use demonstrations*). Morgan was especially excited about making the coins for the cash register. She came to school and said, "Mrs. Wilson, I made George Washingtons and Abraham Lincolns for our cash register!" Earlier, I had shown the children the birthdays of the former presidents on the February calendar, and when I heard Morgan's words, I realized she was making a connection between an earlier learning experience and the coins. The cash register construction included a drawer and a number pad and was used in the dramatic play. The visit to La Mexicana also helped the children understand that they needed math skills in order to exchange money at their class restaurant (PS2: *Introduce modeling and role-play*).

PHASE III: CONCLUDING THE PROJECT

The children were involved in documenting their project as they dictated what was happening in the photos that were taken during the field-site visit. I created a documentation display that included their quotes, and they wanted to invite their families to see the display and have a "restaurant party" (see Figure 6.15). We

Figure 6.13 *(left)* Jorge and Christian attempt to cut shelves that will stay up.

Figure 6.14 *(right)* It took a great deal of experimentation to figure out how to keep the shelves from falling.

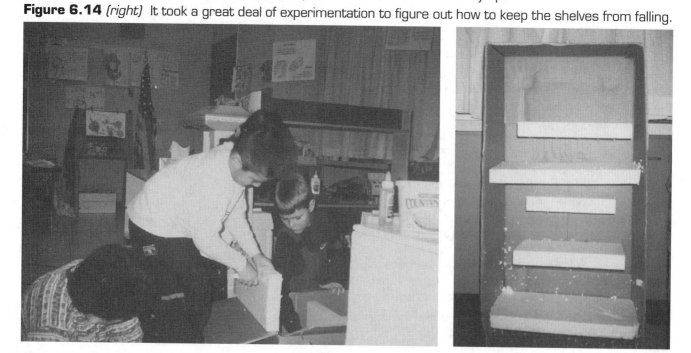

Figure 6.15 Documentation of the children's words and thoughts was displayed at the "restaurant party."

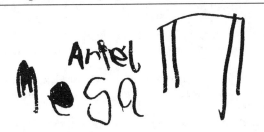

Ariel wrote "mesa" (table) on his own!
¡Ariel escribió la palabra "mesa" solo!

Kennedi wrote, "I like when Joel and Jorge were waiters."

Kennedi escribió, "Me gustó cuando Joel y Jorge eran camareros."

decided to hold a family night (PS7: *Involve parents*). The children discussed who they wanted to invite and made invitations, and La Mexicana provided snacks for the party (see Figure 6.16).

TEACHER REFLECTIONS

The Mexican Restaurant Project enabled the Spanish speakers in my classroom to feel like experts (PS6: *Value native language*). Many of the English- and Spanish-speaking students had eaten in the restaurant, but my Spanish speakers also had experience with the grocery store in La Mexicana because they went there with their parents to buy food. They knew about the products sold in the store the names of these products in Spanish. They were able to ask questions in Spanish and answer many of the English-speaking children's questions, which helped build their self-confidence.

This experience also helped the English-speaking children see the way that learning Spanish can help communication with people in our community.

The restaurant was a great topic for a project. It reflected the culture of my students and their community. Furthermore, it spotlighted a Spanish-speaking family in the community and enabled my students to see Spanish speakers as "experts" (PS6: *Value native language*). The children met many learning goals for kindergarten through the project. They practiced the math skills of writing numerals and using one-to-one correspondence while setting the table. They used letter sounds while writing thank you cards to Jose, and their understanding that print has meaning was reinforced as they made the menus (PS2: *Incorporate modeling and role-play*).

Figure 6.16 The children composed a letter inviting their families to the "restaurant party."

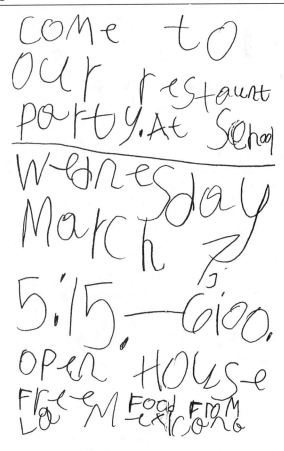

Come to our restaurant party at school!
Wednesday, March 7
5:15–6:00

Open House

Free food from
La Mexicana!

Labeling the food pictures provided practice in learning the alphabet and letter sounds (PS4: *Repeat word and sentence patterns*). The children showed persistence and flexibility in thinking as they planned the grocery store shelves, and they used metacognition as they reflected on and described their visit to La Mexicana.

Perhaps the most meaningful aspect of this project was the way a business in the West Liberty community embraced the project approach. When Jose Elizondo demonstrated how to take an order, he actually sent an order back to the kitchen for a quesadilla for each child. He was not a parent of a child in our class, yet he wanted to support the learning that was taking place. It was wonderful to see everyone work together for the education of our children.

This project also reminded me of the importance of observing children's behavior in the classroom and reflecting their interests in the topics we choose to study. I saw that the children were more interested in restaurants than the topic of food and changed my plans to reflect their interest. As a result, they were very engaged in this project.

REFERENCES

Antunez, B., & Zelasko, N. (2001, August). *What program models exist to serve English language learners?* (FAQ). Washington, DC: National Clearinghouse for Bilingual Education.

Espinosa, L. M. (1995). *Hispanic parent involvement in early childhood programs* (Non-Classroom Use ERIC Document No. EDO-PS-95-3). Urbana, IL: ERIC Clearinghouse on Elementary and Early Childhood Education.

Goldenberg, C. (1993). The home-school connection in bilingual education. In U. Casanova (Ed.), *Bilingual education: Politics, practice, and research* (pp. 225–50). Chicago: University of Chicago Press.

Helm, J. H., & Katz, L. G. (2001). *Young investigators: The project approach in the early years.* New York: Teachers College Press.

Krashen, S. D. (1996). *Under attack: The case against bilingual education.* Culver City, CA: Language Education Associates.

McLaughlin, B. (1992). *Myths and misconceptions about second language learners: What every teacher needs to unlearn.* Santa Cruz, CA: National Center for Research on Cultural Diversity and Second Language Learning.

McLaughlin, B. (1995). *Fostering second language development in young children: Principles and practices.* Santa Cruz, CA: National Center for Research on Cultural Diversity and Second Language Learning.

Ovando, C. J., & Collier, V. P. (1998). *Bilingual and ESL classrooms: Teaching in multicultural contexts.* Boston: McGraw-Hill.

Peregoy, S., & Boyle, O. (1993). *Reading, writing, and learning in ESL: A resource book for K–8 teachers.* White Plains, NY: Longman.

Reyes, M. d. l. L., & Halcon, J. J. (Eds.). (2000). *The best for our children: Critical perspectives on literacy for Latino students.* New York: Teachers College Press.

Tse, L. (2001). *"Why don't they learn English?": Separating fact from fallacy in the U.S. language debate.* New York: Teachers College Press.

Wong Fillmore, L. (1985). Second language learning in children: A proposed model. In J. Provinzano (Ed.), *Issues in English language development.* Rosslyn, VA: National Clearinghouse for Bilingual Education.

CHAPTER 7

Meeting Standards Effectively

Contributors Judy Harris Helm, Sallee Beneke, and Marilyn Worsley

DEFINING THE CHALLENGE
Judy Harris Helm and Sallee Beneke

The challenges discussed in the previous four chapters are closely related to the topic of this chapter—meeting standards effectively. Schools are struggling to rise to the challenge of supporting children who have special needs, who are second-language learners, who have difficulty learning to read, and who are living in poverty. Because of difficulties meeting these challenges, schools are under great scrutiny. The focus of the fifth and last challenge is the educational process and the accountability of that process.

DEFINING DESIRED OUTCOMES

Two aspects of the push toward identification of standards and assessment of those standards concern educators. The first is the lack of agreement on what is being taught and whether the focus is on learning what needs to be learned. The nation collectively wants to refocus parents and schools on the learning that is occurring in classrooms, to determine what children know, and to think about which knowledge, skills, and dispositions should be developed. How do we know if children are learning what they need to know if we have not agreed on what we should be teaching them?

In the last decade and a half, many early childhood educators focused on the developmental appropriateness of learning experiences and the learning environment. In a response to an inappropriate pushdown of materials and methods from elementary grades, early childhood professionals have paid particular attention to the inappropriateness or appropriateness of what we

do as teachers. In *Developmentally Appropriate Practice* (Bredekamp, 1986), guidelines for teachers were provided based on the developmental characteristics of young children, both age-level and individual characteristics. Nine years later, in *Developmentally Appropriate Practice in Early Childhood Programs*, Bredekamp and Copple (1997) updated these guidelines. In 1995 Bredekamp and Rosegrant discussed curriculum and assessment issues, the appropriateness of the context for learning, and the culture of the child.

Until recently, curriculum content or content knowledge had not been a major focus for early childhood educators. Thus, teachers in preschools had little help in determining what content was worthwhile to teach. Often this void was filled with teacher activity books, holiday units and art activities, and commercial units. Although these were often presented in developmentally appropriate ways (that is, the experiences were age-appropriate, active, hands-on learning experiences) they were not focused necessarily on what was meaningful for children or what was most important for them to know for school success. In many preschool programs and centers, selections of experiences were based on what was cute, what parents would like, or what was easiest to do, rather than on what would help children reach established curriculum goals. Although these learning experiences were not harmful to children, they also did not contribute to meeting the challenges described in the previous chapters. In an early childhood classroom observed by one of us, 21 different Halloween craft activities the children had made were displayed on the bulletin boards around the room. In some cases, the planning and preparation of these kinds of activities become the central focus for the teacher rather than the knowledge, skills, and dispositions of the children.

At the kindergarten and early primary level, teachers were more likely to have a set of goals or objectives; again, however, the focus was not always on the knowledge, skills, and dispositions of the children. In some classrooms, the main goal was to "get through" materials, cover topics, and complete texts, worksheets, or computer programs. Dependence on these materials can result in a teacher feeling like he or she has been successful if the material has been presented and completed. Children requiring different experiences or strategies are not so easily accommodated.

This situation led to the call for standards by professional associations, begun first by the National Council of Teachers of Mathematics and now expanded to every content area. The National Education Goals Panel distinguishes between two types of standards (Bredekamp & Rosegrant, 1995). *Content standards* specify what students should be able to do. *Performance standards* gauge to what degree content standards are met, that is, the skill level or competence of the student. As a result, many of these standards were then incorporated into regulations and legislation for public schools. Many states are establishing standards for prekindergarten programs.

ASSESSING LEARNING

The establishment of standards leads to the second concern: Once we have defined what it is that children should learn, how do we know if they are learning it and if teachers and schools are being effective? How do we know if children are learning if we do not take time to assess their learning and look at each child's individual performance? Meaningful assessment of younger children, however, is a challenge within itself because of the ways children learn during the early years. Most early childhood teachers are aware of the importance of active, engaged, meaningful learning experiences and of children constructing their own knowledge through interaction with their environment and others. The work of Piaget (Opper, Ginsberg, & Opper Brandt, 1987) has demonstrated the importance of sensory experiences and concrete learning activities. The NAEYC (1990) confirmed the importance of direct, firsthand, interactive experiences in early childhood education. Active, hands-on learning cannot be easily assessed through standardized, group-administered achievement tests, especially with children who are not yet proficient in reading and writing. Concerns about the introduction of standards into early childhood programs and schools appear to center on how the learning will be assessed:

The pressure to demonstrate effectiveness through children's performance on standardized tests not only changes how teachers teach and what children study, but also seems to be changing our very understanding of the nature of learning and achievement. Group-administered tests focus on the acquisition of simple facts, low-level skills, superficial memorization, and isolated evidence of achievement. The tests hold great power, and that power can be abused. Of greatest concern is that they rob teachers of their sense of judgment about how to help children develop to their optimal potential. (Meisels, 1995, p. 1).

The challenge for teachers of young children, then, becomes determining what to teach and how to assess children's progress in appropriate ways—in other words, how to determine effectiveness in developmentally appropriate and engaging classrooms.

PRACTICAL STRATEGIES
Sallee Beneke

PERSONAL REFLECTIONS

I initially resented as intrusive the implementation of state-mandated standards for early childhood education in the program that I direct. For me, as for many other teachers, the classroom is a place where my staff and I do our best to transform theory into practice. Our classroom is a concrete manifestation of our ideas about teaching and learning. We choose the combination of environment and activities that we believe will best meet the educational needs of the children in our classroom, both individually and as a group. Consequently, when I first learned that Illinois was planning to implement standards for early childhood classrooms, I was protective of our program. We had been using the project approach and the Work Sampling Assessment System at our center for six years, and I thought we were doing an effective job of linking curriculum and assessment to meet the needs of individual children. I feared that these new standards would focus classroom study on discrete skills and segmented bits of knowledge. After examining the Illinois Early Learning Standards, however, I recognized that they supported children's need for active, engaged, and meaningful learning. I have come to see that such standards, when designed and used appropriately (Bowman, Donovan, & Burns, 2000), can fit comfortably within a child-sensitive approach to curriculum planning, such as the project approach, and can raise the quality of education. The standards provide teachers with guidance about what content is considered age-appropriate and important for their students to learn, while the project approach provides a context in which children are motivated to learn and apply this content in a way that is integrated and meaningful.

Figure 7.1 This branch of the anticipatory web from the Pizza Project helped teachers think about pizza ingredients that might be studied.

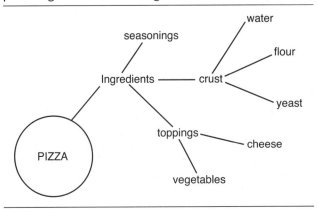

MAXIMIZING THE BENEFITS OF PROJECT WORK

Practical Strategy 1: Plan to Meet the Standards

While the project approach is not a curriculum (Helm & Katz, 2001), it has the potential to offer children many opportunities to meet standards for knowledge, skills, and dispositions. Teacher anticipation and related planning can greatly enhance this potential. First, teachers should encourage children to investigate topics that have potential for developing and applying skills across the curriculum. For example, as Marilyn Worsley explains below, the teachers at our center selected pizza from several other topics that were suggested by the children because they felt it had the most potential to provide experiences in all domains of learning. The teachers knew that the children would have many opportunities to apply and expand on current knowledge, skills, and dispositions, and they could see the possibility for further learning to develop.

Second, teachers need to anticipate what the children might learn in their investigation. Creating a web that includes all that could possibly be learned about the topic is a very useful way to organize this information. Helm and Katz (2001) provided a very helpful description of the process of creating an anticipatory web in *Young Investigators*. When two or more teachers are planning together, the group webbing process described by Chard (1998) can also be useful. For example, the teachers and student teachers at the Illinois Valley Center created an anticipatory web of the Pizza Project that included a branch on ingredients. A simplified version of this branch is presented in Figure 7.1.

As the teachers continued to add to the web of pizza ingredients, they began to anticipate what might be learned if the children's interest developed in this direction, and this potential learning was added to the original web. Zooming in even further on a narrower portion of the web helps to illustrate this process (see Figure 7.2).

Adding benchmarks or standards to the web helps the teacher anticipate what goals are likely to be met through the course of the project and what learning experiences he or she must plan to provide in addition to the project. Figure 7.3 shows how possible classroom activities focused on benchmarks from the Illinois Early Learning Standards have been added to the web. As teachers familiarize themselves with the benchmarks or standards, this process will become less time consuming and more natural. Keeping a condensed list of the standards in a convenient place is helpful. For example, a list might be kept in the teacher's lesson plan book, another copy might be posted in a visible spot in the classroom, and yet another copy might be posted in the area where staff typically meet for planning activities such as webbing

The webbing process can be taken even further. Lists of materials that will be needed for the various activities can be added, and the teacher can think about how to collect documentation of students meeting the standards. For example, the teacher might plan to have a camera ready to take a picture to document the benchmark, "Use tools for investigation (11.B.Eca)" (see Figure 7.3), and he or she might also plan to photocopy the list of safety rules generated by the children as they engage in this activity, noting each child's contribution to the list. Examples of many of the methods and types of documentation that can be used to demonstrate children's learning can be seen in the description of the Pizza Project below.

Anticipatory webbing is a routine part of planning for project work at the Illinois Valley Center. While it is

Figure 7.2 These additions to the Pizza Project web helped teachers to think about what might be learned from an investigation of pizza ingredients.

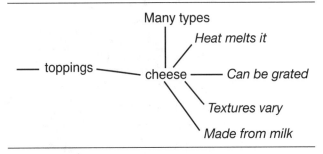

Figure 7.3 The inclusion of benchmarks on the Pizza Project web.

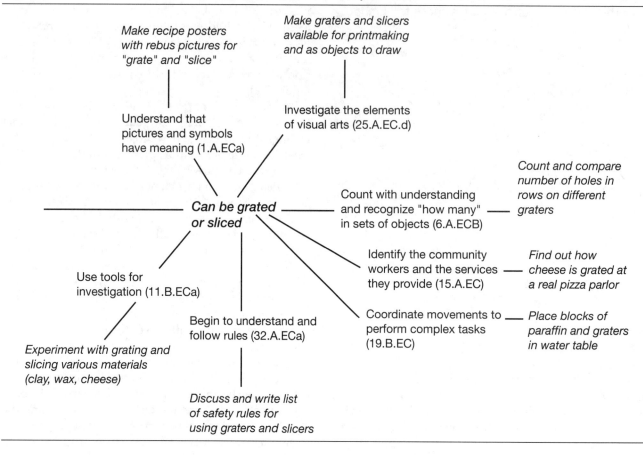

somewhat time consuming, in the larger context it is actually a time saver. The teacher is able to plan for those standards that are not likely to be met in the project, potential activities are identified, lists of materials needed can be generated, and useful methods of documenting learning can be identified and planned. For those teachers who are not comfortable with webbing, a simple table can be used to anticipate the same elements that were explored in the anticipatory web (see Figure 7.4). Although this format is not as flexible as a web, it may be a preferred way for some teachers to

begin thinking about the potential to meet standards in project work.

It is also helpful to make use of a digital camera. Photos can be organized and updated on the computer regularly; while establishing a routine to digest and organize documentation of project work can take some time and effort to get started, it can be very beneficial when it is time to prepare final portfolios of the children's work and summarize their learning.

Many organizers and time savers can be created using a copy machine. For example, before a field-site

Figure 7.4 Although this format is not as flexible as a web, it can be used to anticipate potential learning and standards that may be met in the investigation of a particular topic.

Topic content	What the children might learn	What benchmark might be met	What activities might be planned	Materials to gather	Method of documen-tation

visit, the teacher can photocopy a series of pages including the child's name, the date, and the site that will be visited. The teacher can place these pages in each child's clipboard with the plain side up for the child's drawings. Time that might otherwise have been spent sorting through and labeling children's work can be spent evaluating what was learned and planning further learning experiences.

In summary, it is helpful to teachers who want to explore the potential of a project to meet standards to

1. Familiarize oneself with the standards
2. Select a topic with potential to meet standards across the curriculum
3. Create a web that anticipates all that might be learned through a study of this topic
4. Create a web that identifies the benchmarks or standards that could be met through the project.
5. Add activities that will interest children and support them in achieving the benchmarks identified to the web
6. Add materials and contacts that children may need to implement these activities to the web
7. Add resources that will be needed to document the learning that may take place to the web
8. Take the webbing process deeper as the children's investigation narrows
9. Maximize the potential of the equipment available to develop organizers and time savers
10. Have a routine and system in place for digesting and organizing documentation of achievements

Practical Strategy 2:
Keep the Context of the Work Meaningful

Children have a natural drive to make sense out of their world, and they are more likely to acquire and practice new knowledge, skills, or dispositions that have been set as standards when they need to use them in the course of satisfying their natural curiosity. Learning this way makes sense to them on a personal level, so they are motivated to do their best work. The project approach provides a context that allows the teacher to plan activities that respond to and build on children's interests. By observing children when they are engaged in project work, the teacher is able to see which standards or benchmarks have been achieved and which require further support. Providing this context begins in Phase I and continues throughout the project. Often, the topic of a project emerges as the teacher observes the children in play. For example, musical instruments were selected as a topic for a project at our center after the teachers observed that many of the children enjoyed pretending to play instruments in dramatic play.

It makes sense that the most meaningful learning experiences are those that the child has a hand in planning or developing. In project work, children have the opportunity to guide the direction of the project through their questions and active investigation. For example, in the Musical Instruments Project, the teachers brought in many instruments for the children to examine and incorporate into their play. It became apparent that the children were most interested in guitars and other stringed instruments, so the topic was narrowed to guitars. Eventually, each child designed and constructed his or her own guitar. While the children shared an interest in guitars, their individual constructions expressed their own interests. For example, one little girl said, "See mine. It's a princess guitar!" In the course of this project, children worked in all the domains of learning and met or exceeded many benchmarks.

Practical Strategy 3:
Connect Learning

The project approach can help children see the interconnection of learning, both within and across domains. Likewise, they can often see the connection of their learning to the real world as they are naturally challenged to solve problems within the project. To make these kinds of connections, children need the support of teachers who anticipate the potential learning embedded in the problems encountered by the children and recognize the standards that may be met. For example, when the children said that they would like to make their own guitars, the teachers saw the potential problems that the children would have to solve in the course of the construction. The teachers recognized that as the children solved these problems they would have to draw on knowledge and skills that represent benchmarks from several domains. A list of some of the possible problems and corresponding domains of learning and benchmarks from the *Illinois Early Learning Standards* (Illinois State Board of Education, 2002) include

- Where can I look at real guitars? *Social Science 15.A.EC: Identify the community workers and the services they provide* (p. 22)
- How can I build something that will make a sound like a guitar? *Science 11.A.Eca: Uses senses to explore and observe materials and natural phenomena* (p. 17)
- How can I make a plan for my guitar? *Language Arts 3.C.EC: Use drawing and writing to convey meaning and information* (p. 10)
- How can I make the parts fit together? *Math 7.C.Eca: Demonstrate a beginning understanding of measurement using non-standard units and measurement words* (p. 13)

- How do I use a saw to cut the pieces? *Physical Development 19.B.EC: Coordinate movements to perform complex tasks* (p. 24)
- How can I make the screws go into the wood and attach the wires? *Physical Development 19.B.EC: Coordinate movements to perform complex tasks* (p. 24)
- How can I have the patience to work on this project over time? *Social/Emotional Development 31.A.ECc: Exhibit persistence and creativity in seeking solutions to problems* (p. 31)
- How should I decorate my guitar? *Fine Arts 25.A.ECd: Investigate the elements of the visual arts* (p. 28)
- How can I explain to the adults in my classroom what I want to do? *Language Arts 4.B.EC: Communicate needs, ideas, and thoughts and respond to questions* (p. 11)

As teachers evaluate the potential of a topic to engage children's thinking and stimulate learning, it is helpful to consider the domains of learning, as well as the potential interconnectedness of these domains, that the child might experience in the course of experimenting and problem solving in a project on this topic.

Practical Strategy 4:
Link Curriculum and Assessment

When early childhood teachers think about incorporating standards into their programs, they often wonder how to plan to meet the standards without sacrificing quality. In order to plan experiences that will continue to stimulate development, we need to assess children's growth and learning based on what is taking place in the life of the classroom. In general, curriculum-embedded assessments, such as the Work Sampling System, that consist of ongoing classroom observations of the child are more likely to give accurate results than on-demand assessments such as standardized tests (Meisels, 1995). Likewise, samples of work that have been created by the child under typical classroom circumstances are more likely to be representative of the child's abilities than on-demand assessments.

Inappropriate assessment practices can be avoided when teachers observe and document what children say, do, and produce as they are engaged in classroom activities that are interesting to them. Children's progress and performance on the standards is best documented using an assessment system that is aligned with these standards. For example, Illinois has aligned the Work Sampling System with its standards for young children (Illinois State Board of Education, 2001).

Practical Strategy 5:
Individualize Teaching

There is a beneficial relationship between the project approach and authentic assessments such as the Work Sampling Assessment System. Project work provides many opportunities for teachers to observe what children say and do and to collect samples of the children's work. For example, during the Meadow Project, three children conducted a survey to see which of three insects adults preferred. Two of the children were four years old, and one was three. As they traveled around our building asking people to state their preferences, I observed that the three-year-old boy was making tally marks in the columns of the survey paper, while the two four-year-old girls assisted him by opening doors and holding the clipboard. When the survey was completed, he counted the tally marks and represented each total with a numeral. By observing his behavior and looking at his work, I knew that his math concepts and skills were more advanced than those of many other three-year-olds in the class. I was able to plan experiences that would challenge his growing ability to work with quantities and numerals, and I recognized his interest in creating graphic organizers. In a curriculum in which the teacher plans activities based on typical development for a particular age level, it is difficult to identify and respond to the individual abilities and interests of children who are performing significantly above or below this level. This difficulty is complicated by the fact that a child can be performing at a nontypical level in one or more domains of learning. As teachers, we owe it to children to plan instruction that challenges their growing abilities. It is not enough to have a child meet a particular benchmark or standard; we must be able to help the child learn something new.

Practical Strategy 6:
Support Children's Motivation to Achieve

Children are more likely to apply knowledge and skills spontaneously when they are engaged in project work. Teachers can observe what children understand about how and when to use their knowledge and skills as well as the level at which the children perform when highly motivated. The results of this type of assessment can let teachers know how children are progressing toward meeting standards and then can be used to inform their teaching. The teacher will understand what each child already knows and can do and what the child is starting to learn. Experiences and materials that build on this new learning can be incorporated into the project or taught in addition to it. In this way, teachers can raise the quality of the educa-

Figure 7.5 Children in Jean Thieman's K–1 classroom experiment independently with water pressure as part of the Water to River Project.

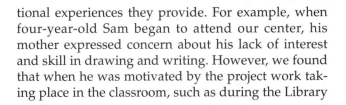

tional experiences they provide. For example, when four-year-old Sam began to attend our center, his mother expressed concern about his lack of interest and skill in drawing and writing. However, we found that when he was motivated by the project work taking place in the classroom, such as during the Library

Figure 7.6 Children are challenged and engaged as they conduct an experiment to see what makes a strong bridge during the Water to River Project.

Project, Sam was interested and capable of writing and drawing. After several visits to the library, some of the children decided to construct a library in our dramatic play area. Sam volunteered to construct the computer. Eventually, the children and teachers moved the library construction to the real library for display. Sam insisted on labeling each part of the computer so viewers would understand what the construction represented. He asked a teacher to write, and then he copied them to make his own labels for the words *monitor*, *CPU*, and *printer*.

The project approach enables teachers to honor children's individual interests and abilities while still providing experiences that challenge them to meet or exceed the standards for their age level. As children engage in project work, they are intrinsically motivated to do their best work (see Figures 7.5 and 7.6).

CONCLUSION

While the advent of standards at the early childhood level presents a new challenge to early childhood educators, it also offers positive possibilities for young children. First, if paired with a child-sensitive curriculum, such as the project approach, and assessed with a method that is curriculum embedded, standards can raise the quality of education for children across the domains. Second, formal standards in early childhood education may bring constructive dialogue to the field, where the focus and quality of education varies widely. This dialogue may result in a higher level of programming for more children. Useful strategies for meeting standards through the project approach include

1. Plan to meet the standards
2. Keep the context of the work meaningful
3. Connect learning
4. Link curriculum and assessment
5. Individualize teaching
6. Support children's motivation to achieve

The potential concern in accepting the adoption of educational standards for young children is that these standards will lead to a narrow, compartmentalized, lockstep curriculum. If the standards cause implementation of a simplified curriculum, then children likely will miss the opportunity to develop understanding of the rich relationships and connections among ideas and skills. They may not truly understand when or why the concepts or skills should be used. I have heard the Early Learning Standards referred to as a map for children's learning. In keeping with this metaphor, it can be helpful to think of standards as destinations on this map. As with a road map, there are many routes to the same destination. Some routes are not as quick as others, but they offer more scenery and opportunity to learn about the people, cultures, and characteristics of the regions crossed. Travelers on this route have a sense of where they are going and where they have been. They will be more likely to find their way back along this path than if they had taken the quicker, more direct route. Once they have reached their destination, they will likely want to continue this pleasant travel experience. They can plan for new or related destinations and use their prior experiences to help them find new routes. Likewise, there are many types of vehicles that can be used for travel. While a jet may be the fastest mode of travel, it offers a very different kind of perspective and depth of understanding than could be developed on a trip across the same territory by bicycle. As teachers begin to implement standards in early childhood programs, it is important that we continue to provide opportunities for children to experience the journey of learning in depth, to make connections within and across disciplines, and to experience the stimulation and satisfaction of challenges and mastery in learning.

I have put forth the hypothesis that the early learning standards can be met through project work, and the best way to test this is to examine standards in light of a real project. As described in the next part of this chapter, the Pizza Project was developed at Illinois Valley Community College's (IVCC) Early Childhood

Education Center in the spring of 2001. Throughout the Pizza Project, the staff at our center paid attention to what benchmarks of the Early Learning Standards were being met. In the past we had used the Work Sampling System to assess our children in seven domains of learning. Because this system was a major resource for the developers of the Early Learning Standards, we found that achievement of these standards could be planned for and assessed in much the same way that we had been assessing children's learning using the Work Sampling System.

THE PIZZA PROJECT
Marilyn Worsley

The Pizza Project took place at the IVCC Early Childhood Education Center near Oglesby, Illinois. Kathie Zecca and Mary Ann Vollmer, the part-time lead teacher in our program, collaborated with me on this project, along with assistant teachers Veronica Flori, Lupe Granados, and Kaleena Riollano. The Early Childhood Education Center is a licensed child care center open from 7:30 A.M. to 5:30 P.M. year-round. Students, faculty, staff, and community members bring their children to the center. Our multi-age classroom serves children ages three through five. Children's attendance patterns at the center vary; some children attend only one, two, or three days per week. Although our population changes from semester to semester, an average of 30–50% of the children come from low-income families according to the Child Care Food Program guidelines for free and reduced-price lunch.

Our program has many strengths. We have been encouraged and supported by our administration in our efforts to implement the project approach and use documentation practices, including the Work Sampling Assessment System. The project approach and documentation complement each other. The administration supports continuing professional development in the project approach, including participation in the Illinois Project Group. We are also fortunate to have field trip transportation and funds to cover some extra project materials available to us. Another strength for our program is the interest of our parents in our work and the availability of volunteers and extra assistant teachers to assist on field trips. Multi-age grouping is another asset for using the project approach; we always have returning students who have experience with project investigations, and they act as models for the younger children.

Just as the Pizza Project was beginning, I received a draft copy of the new *Illinois Early Learning Standards* (Illinois State Board of Education, 2001). As I looked them over, I was pleased to see that the Work Sampling

System was used as a reference for many of the benchmarks. We had been using this system for several years, and I hoped that this familiarity would help us learn to incorporate the standards into our planning. As we proceeded with the Pizza Project, we decided to look at it through the lens of the new standards to see whether our project-based curriculum would have to be altered.

PHASE I: BEGINNING THE PROJECT

We began the Pizza Project in a way that was new for us. In the past, we usually selected our topic in response to a common interest we noticed building among the children, or we chose a particular topic to see if it would be successful with the children. In the spring of 2001, however, we decided to let the children suggest and vote on a topic for investigation (PS1: *Keep context meaningful*). At a meeting with the children, I asked them for ideas about possible topics we could investigate. The children came up with a variety of possible topics: trucks, calculators, pizza, dinosaurs, our heads,

and cardboard boxes. The list was narrowed through two rounds of voting. Through this process, the children were able to see the usefulness of counting and graphs (PS3: *Connect learning*). First, the teaching staff voted for their top two choices from the original list: trucks and pizza. The next day the children used Post-it notes to cast their votes on a voting graph. They voted to choose between trucks and pizza. Pizza was the winner.

After the votes were counted and pizza was chosen, we gave the children opportunities to share their current knowledge of pizza. We began a web, which we added to over the coming days (see Figure 7.7; PS3: *Connect learning*). An advantage to this topic was that all the children had prior knowledge of pizza. Some talked about going to certain pizza parlors or having pizza delivered for birthday parties. We also arranged our lesson plan so that the children could draw and talk about pizza. Most children created drawings of whole pizzas, while others drew only a specific topping (see Figure 7.8; PS5: *Individualize instruction*).

We wanted to give the children an opportunity to "mess around with the topic" because we hoped to get

Figure 7.7 Web of the children's knowledge of pizza at the beginning of the Pizza Project. Note that the children added quite a bit of information about tools as they had an opportunity to "mess around with the topic."

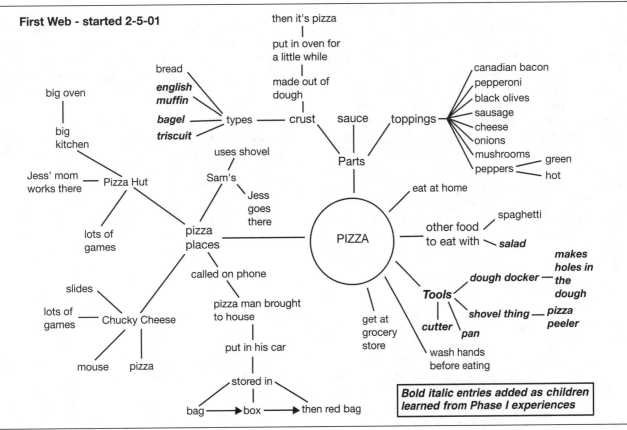

Figure 7.8 Phase I drawings from the Pizza Project capture the children's beginning knowledge about pizza. They also reflect the range of development in the classroom.

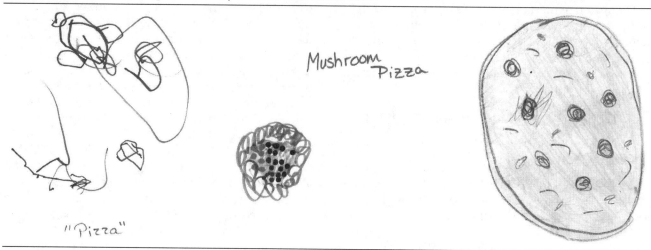

"Pizza"

Mushroom Pizza

a sense of what direction their interests would take the investigation (PS2: *Keep context meaningful*). We often began investigations by encouraging children to explore tools associated with the topic. In this case, we were fortunate to have a part-time assistant teacher, Veronica Flori, who also worked as a manager of Bianchi's, a pizza parlor in nearby Ottawa, Illinois. The owners of Bianchi's were very generous and allowed Veronica to bring in pizza pans, chef hats, and pizza tools, including "dough dockers." Veronica introduced these tools at circle time, and they were placed in the housekeeping area for dramatic play. We also brought in several types of cheese graters and pizza cutters for examination and experimentation. The children felt, drew, constructed, labeled, and used them. They explored pizza toppings by feeling, counting, smelling, cutting, cooking, and watching what happened when they were not refrigerated. Literature about pizza production and delivery was introduced. Many writing and math samples resulted from these Phase I activities. For example, Breanna, who was five, labeled her drawings with the words *rolling pin* and *pizza tray*. Her letters were well formed and uniform in size (see Figure 7.9). Three-year-old Alex also labeled her drawing of a cheese grater. Her writing included letter-like shapes and a reversed *E* (see Figure 7.10). Alex's interest and ability in labeling continued to develop during the Pizza Project. Children often drew collections of tools on one piece of paper (see Figure 7.11; PS4: *Link curriculum and assessment*; PS5: *Individualize instruction*).

We asked the children what they wanted to learn about pizza (PS2: *Keep context meaningful*). We made a list of their questions and placed it on the project history board. More questions were added throughout the project. The original questions were

What is the crust made out of? Bread?
Are there other ways to get pizza besides from a pizza place?
What is the shovel for putting pizzas in the oven?
What do the ovens at pizza places look like?
How does the sauce go from tomato to sauce?
What is the name of people who buy pizza?

Throughout the project, children suggested ideas for further investigation that were inspired by their play and exploration. For example, during an activity in which the children were experimenting with melting cheese, one child suggested that we should try melting

Figure 7.9 Five-year-old Breanna labeled her drawing of the rolling pin.

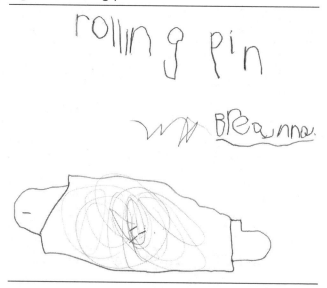

Figure 7.10 Three-year-old Alex drew the cheese grater and labeled her drawing. Note the reversed *E* to the left of the handle.

other cheeses along with the cheese that is usually used on pizza. She wanted to see how the melting process would vary for different cheeses (PS6: *Support motivation to achieve*).

Many of the activities that we developed for Phase I of the Pizza Project met benchmarks of the Illinois Early Learning Standards. Literacy and science skills were especially well covered in this phase. As I learn to incorporate the Early Learning Standards into my planning, I believe it will be helpful to continue to do advance planning and add the standards that may be met to my anticipatory web (PS1: *Plan to meet standards*). An anticipatory web is created for each project that we begin at our center. Until the Pizza Project, however, our webs had only included topic information, potential activities, and possible documentation. By including the benchmarks that may or may not be met in the project, I will be able to judge what activities I need to offer outside of the project. Including the standards in the webbing process helps teachers offer a more complete curriculum.

PHASE II: INVESTIGATION

The children were interested in how pizza is made and the delivery process. They had acted out pizza delivery in the dramatic play area and through a flannelboard version of the story *Hi, Pizza Man!* (Walter, 1998). However, we wanted to give them the opportunity to

experience these processes in a real way. Veronica was able to arrange two field trips to Bianchi's Pizza Parlor. The first visit gave the children an opportunity to look around, observe, and listen to the information shared by the experts. They took clipboards and a few general questions with them. Their questions were well covered in the tour, and their interest seemed to focus in on the machine used to grind meat and cheese and the oven. We thought it would be useful to take an exploratory first trip so that the children would have enough information to fuel their curiosity (PS6: *Support motivation to achieve*).

While they were at Bianchi's, the children saw a large piece of equipment grind up cheese. When we returned to the classroom, we began to talk with them about what they had seen and what they might like to know more about (PS2: *Keep context meaningful*). Prior to the field trip, Veronica made a notebook with labeled photographs of the pizza parlor to give the children an idea of what they might see there. With that book, their experience in dramatic play, and their experience on their first field-site visit as a basis, the children planned their second trip to Bianchi's. They listed the things that they thought they might see there: pizza oven, big refrigerator, food, dough, pin, sauce, cheese, peppers, bologna, kitchen, salads, rolling pins, mandarin oranges, pizza, boxes, mushrooms, pizza pans, sausages, dough docker, Pizza Hut on the way, chef, managers, cooks, sinks, washing machine, buckets for food, rolling mixer, lettuce, and cherries. It was apparent that they already

Figure 7.11 A child's drawing of three pizza tools: the cutter, the edger, and the pan. These sketches were a way for the child to gather information rather than an artistic effort.

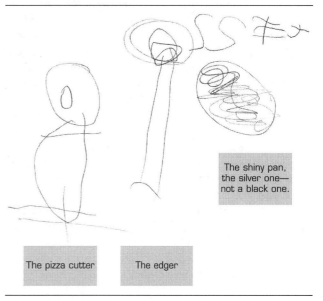

The shiny pan, the silver one— not a black one.

The pizza cutter

The edger

Figure 7.12 Teacher Marilyn Worsley points out details of the grinder machine.

knew quite a bit about the tools, personnel, and operation of the pizza parlor (PS4: *Link curriculum and assessment*), but the second trip truly deepened this understanding and challenged them to learn and use new knowledge, skills, and dispositions (PS6: *Support motivation to achieve*).

The second trip was taken one week later. During this trip many of the children focused on sketching "the grinder," which fascinated them (see Figure 7.12; PS2: *Keep context meaningful*). On the first visit, they saw the grinder pour out buckets of shredded cheese, and on the second visit the grinder was making sausage. Several of the children helped pour the spices into the grinder with the meat. The children were allowed to look into the top of the grinder, and then they watched the sausage come out into buckets that were then loaded onto a rolling cart. Several of the children sketched the grinder. Four-year-old Jess sketched the buckets of food on the cart, tallied the buckets, and used numerals to record the number of buckets (see Figures 7.13 and 7.14; PS3: *Connect learning*). Tallying and writing numerals were new skills for Jess. Learning and applying these skills in an integrated process helped him understand their usefulness (PS5: *Individualize instruction*). Other children sketched the pizza warmer, the large cans on the shelves, the industrial-sized mixer, the sink, and the washing machine. The drain in the floor of the kitchen was very interesting to several children; they drew it and counted the holes (PS6: *Support motivation to achieve*).

Before we left Bianchi's, the children made their own pizzas. They used the same professional tools that Veronica had brought into our dramatic play area: the dough docker, and the edger (see Figure 7.15). Later, Veronica brought our freshly baked pizzas to us at the center. The children were thrilled to eat the pizzas they had made themselves at the real pizza parlor (PS3:

Figure 7.13 Four-year-old Jess leans forward to get a better view of the grinder machine.

Figure 7.14 Jess sketched the rolling cart and tallied the bins on the shelves and the buckets on the cart. He counted the tally marks and wrote the numeral to represent the quantity.

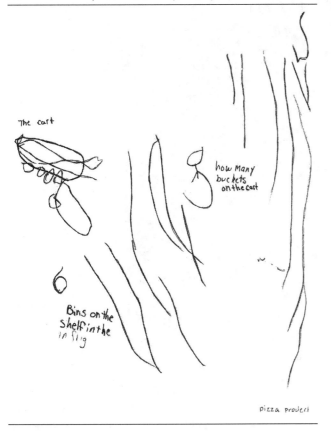

ers on the grinder. It was interesting to watch the problem solving and learning that went into this construction (PS4: *Link curriculum and assessment*). I suggested that they look at the photographs of the grinder in the album of pictures from Veronica. They used these photos to draw plans for their construction (PS3: *Connect learning*).

Among the materials we had gathered to use in the construction were several large cardboard boxes. I assumed that the grinder team would take one of the boxes and cut holes in it to represent the openings in the real grinder. Instead they used a saw to cut the four sides of the box apart. Then they used a tape measure as part of their discussion about the proper height of the grinder. Robbie used a yardstick to draw a strip of paper that was the correct length, and they used it as a pattern for the height of their construction. Connecting all the pieces of cardboard was a challenge. They tried several methods, including white school glue, before they settled on masking tape. During the process of taping the grinder together, they discovered that it worked best if one person held the pieces while another applied the tape. I was really impressed with their determination and skill in assembling the grinder. They sawed, cut, taped, stapled, drew, painted, and folded. At first glance, the finished product looked like a funny old box covered with tape and with the bottom of a plastic water cooler jug sticking out of it. On closer examination, however, a great deal of detail could be seen in this construction. The boys even made holes in the top of the grinder so the spices could be added, as they saw on the real one.

Numerous learning standards were met during Phase II of the Pizza Project (PS4: *Link curriculum and assessment*). Language arts, social science, mathematics, and social/emotional development were prominent in this phase. In the area of language arts, we saw the children practice writing letters as they made labels for their drawings and constructions. I was very pleased to watch the progress of a three-year-old who, over the course of this project, went from not even writing his name to writing *meat grinder* for a label. In the area of social science, the children gained deep understanding of the workings and value of a community business. In math, they had many opportunities to apply measurement and number concepts in a meaningful context. They became more aware of geometric shapes, experimented with three-dimensional objects, formed patterns, and made predictions. The children also demonstrated that they had met the social/emotional standards set by the Illinois Early Learning Standards (2002). For example, the team that constructed the grinder was eager and curious about learning how to put together their construction (p. 32); persistent and

Connect learning). In the following days, we were able to revisit the pizza parlor using a videotape made during the trip.

After the children returned from the trip, we made a list of what we had seen (PS3: *Connect learning*). The children had previously started to convert the dramatic play area into a pizza parlor. Just as I had predicted, when they returned from the trip they said they wanted to make their pizza parlor more like Bianchi's. They dictated a list of the items they wanted to construct (PS6: *Support motivation to achieve*). We discussed what to make first, who would work on each part, and what materials we might need (PS3: *Connect learning*). The two pieces of equipment that the children actually finished constructing were a grinder and a pizza warmer. Although children drifted in and out of different work groups, core teams of children seemed to stick with each construction. While the construction of the pizza warmer by three-year-olds Kylie and Alex was interesting, I will discuss the construction of the grinder in detail. Jess, Robbie, and Justin were the primary work-

Figure 7.15 Justin docks the dough at Bianchi's Pizza Parlor.

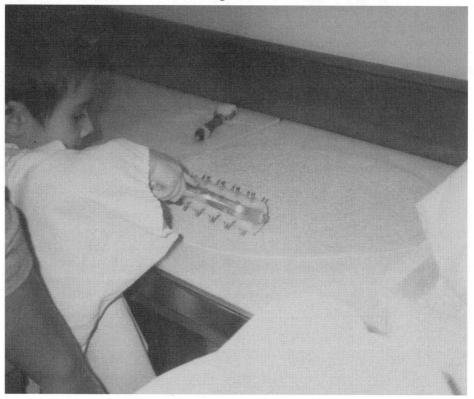

showed initiative (p. 32); able to work as a team and express their frustrations appropriately (p. 31); and so intent on their work that transitions or rules were never an issue (p. 31). They truly came to think of themselves as a team, and I think the bond that was created through this construction continued after the project ended (p. 32). In their work together they communicated their ideas freely (p. 31) and were considerate of each other's feelings (p. 32).

PHASE III: CONCLUDING THE PROJECT

As the constructions were completed, the semester at IVCC was also coming to a close. Together with the children, we decided to have a pizza party to celebrate the end of the semester and to show families what the children had learned during the course of the Pizza Project. Planning for this party became yet another opportunity for the children to engage in problem solving (PS3: *Connect learning*). We charted how many people from each family would be coming, what type of pizza they liked to eat, and the number of slices of pizza they usually ate to determine how many pizzas to order. It was exciting to see how well the children anticipated the types and amounts of pizza that we would need for our party.

We had a huge turnout for this event, and I think the parents were truly impressed with the children's work. The families ate Bianchi's pizza, watched the video of the field trip, and looked at displays of the children's drawings, paintings, writing, and constructions. Before the party, the children dictated a list of their work from the Pizza Project that they wanted to be sure their families would see. I think that making this list helped the children to reflect on all the places they had visited, representations they had created, and experiments in which they had participated (PS3: *Connect learning*). It also helped remind them to take their parents to see the work that was displayed in all the areas in the classroom. The pizza party was a wonderful culmination to the project.

TEACHER REFLECTIONS

In this project, as in all the others that I have experienced, I was a co-learner. I believe that in order to help the children learn and investigate in a project, it is essential for me to look at the world with the same sense of wonder and excitement as them. Sharing my genuine interest and enjoyment in learning about the topic is a powerful teaching tool. I think that pizza was a great topic for a project. The children already had some basic knowledge about it, so they could relate it

Figure 7.16 Examples of the ways children met math benchmarks through activities from the Pizza Project.

Math Benchmarks from the Illinois Early Learning Standards	Activities from the Pizza Project
6.A.Eca. Use concepts that include number recognition, counting, and one-to-one correspondence	• Made field sketches of kitchen tools and equipment • Played numeral match game (matched numeral to slices of pizza with varying number of pepperoni) • Used simple recipes and recipe posters to cook pizza
6.A.Ecb. Count with understanding and recognize "how many" in sets of objects	• Counted wheels on a cart at Bianchi's Pizza Parlor and recreated the cart in the classroom • Used tallies to count things observed during field work, such as the number of buckets of sausage and the number of wheels on the cart
6.B.EC. Solve simple mathematical problems	• Decided how long pieces of cardboard and paper should be in constructing models of the pizza warmer and meat/cheese grinder • Decided how many pizzas to order for family pizza party
6.C.ECa. Explore quantity and number	• Played numeral match game (matched numeral to slices of pizza with varying number of pepperoni) • Made tally marks on field drawings to record buckets, cans, and wheels seen at Bianchi's • Used measuring tape to construct pizza warmer and cheese/sausage grinder • Decided how many pizzas to order for family pizza party
6.C.Ecb. Connect number words to quantities they represent using physical models and representations	• Voted for topic and recorded votes on voting chart • Used measuring tape to construct pizza warmer and cheese/sausage grinder • Decided how many pizzas to order for family pizza night • Played numeral match game (matched numeral to slices of pizza with varying number of pepperoni) • Used a recipe to determine quantities to be measured and added to make pizza dough and sauce
6.D.EC. Make comparisons of quantities	• Voted for topic and recorded votes on voting chart • Grated piles of paraffin at the water table and compared sizes of piles • Tallied the types of pizza for family pizza night
7.A.Eca. Demonstrate a beginning understanding of measurement using nonstandard units and measurement words	• Used a tape measure to determine the number of inches in length of a paper pattern for the pizza warmer

Figure 7.16 *Continued.*

Math Benchmarks from the Illinois Early Learning Standards	Activities from the Pizza Project
7.A.Ecb. Construct a sense of time through participation in daily activities	• Took part in an extended project and planning and building multi-stage constructions (meat grinder, pizza warmer) • Made and implemented plans for family pizza night
7.B.EC. Show understanding of and use comparative words	• Grated piles of paraffin at the water table and compared sizes of piles • Discussed voting chart and decided which topic had more votes • Discussed how tall and wide the pizza warmer and sausage/cheese grater should be • Built a pizza warmer and sausage/cheese grater using pre-determined measurements
7C.Eca. Use tools to measure	• Measured to construct pizza warmer and sausage/cheese grater using yard stick and tape measure
7.C.Ecb. Incorporate estimating and measuring activities into play	• Grated paraffin at the water table and measured it with dry measuring cups and measuring spoons • Used recipes, measuring cups, pizza pans, and bowls in dramatic play area
8.A.EC. Sort and classify objects by a variety of properties	• Made a pizza collage at art table • Played a vegetable "feely game" • Played with flannelboard pizza and flannel ingredients • Guessed pizza ingredients based on their smell
8.B.Eca. Recognize, duplicate, and extend simple patterns, such as sequences of sounds and other shapes	• Read along with predictable books, such as *Hi, Pizza Man!* • Drew pizza tools, such as graters with rows of holes and dockers with sets of prongs
8.C.EC. Solve problems using systems of numbers and their properties	• Decided how many pizzas to order for family pizza party
8.D.EC. Describe qualitative change, such as growing taller	• Experimented with yeast and the way it causes dough to rise • Observed that rotting tomatoes grew flatter • Noted changes in pizza ingredients when baked (cheese melted and bubbled, crust turned brown)

Figure 7.16 *Continued.*

Math Benchmarks from the Illinois Early Learning Standards	Activities from the Pizza Project
9.B.EC. Find and name locations with simple relationships such as "near"	• Discussed what was seen on the field trip to Bianchi's Pizza Parlor • Planned placement of items in classroom pizza parlor for dramatic play • Discussed photographs of equipment and work areas in Bianchi's Pizza Parlor
10.A.Eca. Represent data using concrete objects, pictures, and graphs	• Voted for topic and recorded votes on voting chart • Tallied wheels and containers in field sketches • Sketched what was seen on field-site visit • Drew pizza tools • Sculpted clay models of pizza tools • Drafted plans for construction of the pizza warmer and sausage/cheese grinder • Graphed what kind of pizza each family eats and how many slices each family member would likely eat at the pizza party
10.A.Ecb. Make predictions about what will occur	• Predicted what would happen if tomatoes were left out, and then tested the hypothesis by rotting the tomatoes • Predicted what would happen when cheese was heated in the oven
10.B.EC. Pose questions and gather data about themselves and their surroundings	• Predicted what they might see at Bianchi's Pizza Parlor • Developed questions to ask on field trip to Bianchi's • Drew field sketches of tools, equipment, and supplies at Bianchi's

to their own lives. There were many opportunities for hands-on learning experiences with real artifacts that the children could manipulate, and it provided avenues for learning about the community. It also provided many opportunities for representation through drawing, painting, construction, and drama. I was pleased that we were able to observe many instances of the children meeting the Illinois Early Learning Standards in all domains of learning. The Pizza Project was especially helpful in meeting math and science benchmarks (see Figure 7.16).

Looking at this project through the lens of the new Illinois Early Learning Standards has helped me to think about how to plan activities with these standards in mind. In the future, I will continue to incorporate planning to meet the standards into the webbing I do in anticipation of a project. As I become more familiar with these standards, I believe that our use of the project approach will help us meet them.

REFERENCES

Bowman, B. T., Donovan, M. S., and Burns, M. S. (Eds.). (2000). *Eager to learn.* Washington, D.C.: National Academy Press.

Bredekamp, S. (Ed.). (1986). *Developmentally appropriate practice.* Washington, DC: National Association for the Education of Young Children.

Bredekamp, S., & Copple, C. (Eds.). (1997). *Developmentally appropriate practice in early childhood programs* (Rev. ed.). Washington, DC: National Association for the Education of Young Children.

Bredekamp, S., & Rosegrant, T. (1995). *Reaching potentials: Transforming early childhood curriculum and assessment* (Vol. 2). Washington, DC: National Association for the Education of Young Children.

Chard, S. C. (1998). *The project approach: A practical guide 1.* New York: Scholastic.

Helm, J. H., and Katz, L. (2001). *Young investigators: The project approach in early childhood education.* New York: Teachers College Press.

Illinois State Board of Education. (2001). *Work sampling assessment, Illinois: Preschool–4 guidelines.* New York: Rebus, Inc.

Illinois State Board of Education, Division of Early Childhood. (2002). *Illinois early learning standards.* Springfield, IL: Illinois State Board of Education.

Meisels, S. J. (1995). *Performance assessment in early childhood education: The work sampling system. ERIC digest.* Urbana, IL: ERIC Clearinghouse on Elementary and Early Childhood Education.

National Association for the Education of Young Children. (1990). Guidelines for appropriate curriculum content and assessment in programs serving children ages 3 through 8. In S. Bredekamp & T. Rosegrant (Eds.), *Reaching potentials: Appropriate curriculum and assessment for young children* (Vol. 2). Washington, DC: National Association for the Education of Young Children.

Opper, S., Ginsberg, H. P., & Opper Brandt, S. (1987). *Piaget's theory of intellectual development.* Englewood Cliffs, NJ: Prentice Hall, Inc.

Walter, V. (1998). *Hi, Pizza Man!* New York: Orchard Press.

CHAPTER 8

The Importance of Documentation

Judy Harris Helm

Documentation is an important part of project work. Viewing displays of children's work often inspires teachers to begin using the project approach in their own classrooms. The schools of Reggio Emilia, Italy, are well known for their professionally prepared artistic displays of children's project work. Display is not the sole or even the most important use of documentation, however; documentation informs educators about children's learning and provides evidence for making decisions. Project documentation, or evidence of the learning that occurs through project work, takes many forms, including narratives of the project and children's products, observations, portfolios, and reflections (Helm, Beneke, & Steinheimer, 1998). One of the most valid reasons for spending time and effort on documentation is the way that it can shape teaching.

REFLECTIVE PRACTICE

When Rebecca Wilson, the co-author of Chapter 6, was in high school, she spent part of a summer volunteering in a classroom at the Valeska Hinton Early Childhood Education Center. It was then that she discovered her love for teaching and decided to become a bilingual early childhood teacher. As she spent time in the classroom interacting with the children and observing teacher Beth Crider-Olcott, she shared a 16-year-old's reflections on teaching:

You know some people say that teaching early childhood is easy. All you do is play with children. It isn't. I watch Beth teach, and I think she is actually doing two jobs and she does it in two places at one time. One job is when she is down on the floor and she is keeping track of children, organizing activities, knowing who is in the bathroom and who needs to go there, filling up the easel paints. But then she is doing another job. This job is like she is on the ceiling looking down. In this job she is observing and analyzing, figuring out who knows what and who is struggling to figure something out. She is thinking what she can do next to help children learn.

We began to call this second job "ceiling work," and it includes all of the reflective work that teachers do: setting goals, observing, assessing, and adjusting their support and guidance to the needs of each child. It is through ceiling work that teachers examine and reexamine the meaningfulness of learning experiences for young children, the effectiveness of their practices, and the long-term impact of classroom activities on children's development. We also determine how to provide meaningful and productive experiences that build knowledge, skills, and dispositions and that make good use of child and teacher time.

Meaningful Planning

Teachers who use the project approach to meet the challenges described in this book do much ceiling work. Although good project work often appears to observers as child driven and effortless on the part of the teacher, there is much that teachers do to keep project work meaningful for children. Throughout the descriptions of the projects in this book, teachers made a number of references to planning that occurred for project work. In Chapter 7, Sallee Beneke described the use of the anticipatory planning web as a way to incorporate standards in projects. This process is described in greater detail in *Young Investigators* (Helm & Katz, 2001). Often, teachers are surprised at the introduction of such an organized planning process to a dynamic learning experience like projects. One of the characteristics of the project approach, however, is that it provides a structure for doing projects with children, including the preliminary planning (Chard, 1998; Helm & Katz, 2001; Katz & Chard, 1989). By carefully thinking about the content and concepts inherent in the topic and how required curriculum and assessment can be integrated, teachers can maximize the learning experiences of children.

Teaching and Responding

Planning is a type of ceiling work usually done in a formal way before projects begin. Often it occurs by teams of teachers. However, the formality of the anticipatory planning web does not mean that the progression of the project is predetermined or that the web becomes an outline or plan of action that the teacher and children will then plow through. As the topic is explored and children begin to develop questions for investigation, documentation becomes a key part of the project process. Documentation of children's work, thoughts, and reactions helps teachers guide projects. A teacher may observe a child's surprise when there are not enough menus in the pretend restaurant for all of the customers. She may make a note of this emerging understanding of the importance of one-to-one correspondence. Then she may ask the child how he can figure out how many more menus are needed. This dynamic, flexible approach to instruction, which occurs in the daily progress of a project, is often called "teaching on the fly" (Helm & Katz, 2001). The teacher makes many decisions while in the midst of observing children's interactions in the classroom, asking children questions, responding to their questions, and facilitating the work in process. It is this spontaneity that preserves the elements of self-initiation and self-direction in project work, which are so beneficial to the development of children's dispositions, resiliency, and self-confidence.

Of course, teaching on the fly does not require anticipatory planning, and many teachers do an excellent job without it. Some observers may be concerned that the formalization of ceiling work in anticipatory planning webs and other planning devices reduces the spontaneity or flexibility of "true project work." In schools where teachers face major challenges, however, they, along with parents and administrators, want to maximize the benefits of project work for developing required knowledge and skills. By thinking in advance about how required curriculum can be integrated and then relying on documentation to reveal the appropri-

ate timing for integration, the teacher can accomplish many goals during project work and still maintain the spontaneity of the project.

This integration also enables teachers to justify taking time out of busy schedules for project work. Rather than having to teach required skills during separate, isolated experiences, the teacher can integrate them into project work and capitalize on the usefulness of such skills as data collection and reading and writing. When teachers think carefully in advance about the possibilities for integrating standards, assessment, and individual educational goal, they are often able, on the fly, to ask questions, suggest data collection, or challenge a child to problem solve at the precise moment that it appears most useful and relevant to the child. This is especially beneficial to children who have not had an opportunity to observe the important relevant uses of literacy or mathematical problem solving within the home environment. A key part of ceiling work and effective teaching on the fly, however, is effective use of documentation.

PURPOSES OF DOCUMENTATION

There is a strong relationship between good project work and good documentation, although there are many different ways to record and share. Some of the purposes of documentation are guiding instruction, individual child assessment, studying pedagogy, and communication about the educational process. In classrooms where teachers are facing challenges, many, if not all, of these uses of documentation may occur.

Guiding Instruction

Because projects progress according to children's interest and needs, teachers need an accurate way to gather information about what children are doing, what they are asking, and what they are thinking during the progress of the project. Documentation for guiding instruction is ongoing, and reflection on the documentation is usually immediate. Teachers listen, observe, and examine children's work. They may make anecdotal notes, take digital photographs. They may collect and carefully examine children's products, such as drawings and constructions, that are produced during the day or over a short period of time. This documentation is often referred to as raw or unprocessed documentation, and it is used immediately. What the teacher and his or her colleagues gain is a sense of where the project might go next, what materials and resources it might be helpful to introduce, and how to shape their own interactions with the children. Documentation for guiding instruction is part of teachers' ceiling work and enables teaching on the fly to be productive and effective. Teachers may or may not choose to share this raw documentation with others, such as parents or members of the school community.

Child Assessment

Documentation can also be used to assess the development of the knowledge, skills, and dispositions of an individual child. When teachers face the challenges discussed in this book, individual child assessment enables the teacher to be sure that each child is learning what he or she needs to learn to be successful in school. Assessment tells the teacher what each child does and does not know and can and cannot do. As pointed out in Chapter 7, the most appropriate type of assessment for young children is authentic performance assessment, that is, assessment that is based on activities that children engage in on a daily basis (Meisels, 1993).

Authentic performance assessment relies on quality documentation, including children's work samples collected into portfolios, photographic or video recordings, and observations captured in anecdotal notes. Often, teachers can use an individual developmental checklist to document the growth and development of skills over a period of time. There are many different approaches to authentic performance assessment, especially for portfolios, that meld nicely with project work (Dichtelmiller et al., 1997; Gardner, 1993; Gronlund & Engel, 2001; Gullo, 1994; Meisels, 1995). Howard Gardner's work on multiple intelligences has resulted in the project spectrum approach, in which assessment activities are embedded in the curriculum (Gullo, 1994).

Systematic and focused authentic performance assessments have been found to be reliable and valid for project work. For example, studies of the Work Sampling System have shown that teacher's judgments of performance using it correlate well with a standardized, individually administered, psycho-educational battery; that it is a reliable predictor of achievement ratings in kindergarten–grade 3; and correctly identify children at risk (Meisels et al, 2001).

Projects offer rich and varied sources of documentation for assessment. Because children are highly engaged and motivated, they put significant effort into their work. Projects also provide a venue for the implementation of academic skills that children are learning in other parts of the curriculum.

Studying Pedagogy

Documentation provides insight into the teaching and learning processes. When documentation is collected and studied for the purpose of understanding these processes, it is sometimes called pedagogical documentation (Dahlberg, Moss, & Pence, 1999). Pedagogical documentation is a major component of the philosophy of schools in Reggio Emilia, where reflection and in-depth documentation shapes their pedagogy and is the major source of professional growth and development (Rinaldi, 2001).

An excellent example of pedagogical documentation in U.S. schools and centers is *Rearview Mirror: Reflections of a Preschool Car Project,* by Sallee Beneke (1998). Through this captivating documentation of the exploration of a car by children in a community college child care center, the reader participates in the reflections of Beneke, the center's staff, parents, and the automotive center's staff where the project took place. The documentation enables teachers to examine the pedagogical decisions made during the project and the value of the learning experiences.

Documentation captures what might otherwise be lost in the busy, demanding pace of the classroom. Figure 8.1 is one of several photos taken by the teacher in a dual-language kindergarten program during a time when children were making their own choices about what they wanted to do. When the teacher viewed the photos later, she noticed how this child not only chose to spend her play time making numbers, but she had great enthusiasm for the task.

Communication

Documentation also can provide a vehicle for communicating about early childhood programs. This communication occurs between staff members, with children about their work, with parents about what is happening in children's classrooms and how their children are learning, and with the members of the greater community. When documentation is used in this way, the teacher is able to open windows into the heart of the classroom and develop respect, understanding, and support for the work being done there (Helm et al., 1998). Unfortunately, few U.S. schools and centers have documenters or individuals with professional training in communication. In Appendix A, Amanda Helm provides some of this expertise in her answer to the question about how a teacher might select documentation. There is much that educators can learn from professional communicators.

DOCUMENTATION AND THE CHALLENGES

Documentation can assist teachers in meeting the challenges outlined in this book. Documentation enables close assessment and monitoring of the development of

Figure 8.1 Bianca's decision to spend playtime writing numbers on the board, and her enthusiasm in doing so, documents a positive disposition toward math and counting.

the knowledge, skills, and dispositions of children. This is especially helpful for meeting the challenges of supporting children's movement toward literacy, and the development of other academic skills as well as learning a second language. Close assessment and monitoring also enables teachers to meet children's special needs and meet standards in effective and appropriate ways.

Parent involvement and participation is encouraged when teachers share documentation. This is especially helpful for overcoming the ill effects of poverty, supporting second-language learners, and meeting children's special needs. Good documentation demonstrates the value of engaged learning experiences and culturally relevant, integrated projects; it also shows parents and the community how they can support and encourage the development of children.

Documentation can play a significant role in supporting the development of resiliency in children. When children see documentation of their work, they see themselves as learners, and when it is shared with parents, they develop an image of the child as resilient and competent. Documentation captures and makes children aware of their own resiliency strategies in working with others, problem solving, and doing things independently.

As documentation of children's learning is shared, members of the school and community begin to see the school as successful and children as learners. When bulletin boards, newsletters, and community displays focus on the development of knowledge, skills, and dispositions instead of holiday themes, the school becomes centered on children's learning. Chapter 7 stated that demand for accountability was a reason for the push toward standards. Documentation enables the teacher to meet some of the concerns that citizens and those outside the immediate community might have about the effectiveness of the school program. When documentation captures the knowledge, skills, and dispositions that are being developed, observers can recognize that the school is preparing productive citizens.

HOW MUCH DOCUMENTATION?

One of the concerns that teachers in U.S. schools and centers have about documentation is how much is necessary to be effective. Teachers who face the challenges discussed in this book are very busy. They are pulled in many directions by the needs of their children and families. It is not uncommon for a teacher in one of these schools to talk to a parent about an adult education program before school, tutor a child during the lunch break, and translate materials for second-language learners after school. Unfortunately, although we wish it were otherwise, many early childhood programs, outside of laboratory schools, do not have extensive time for collegial interaction and reflection.

It is helpful when documentation within project work can be used for multiple purposes. When achievement of standards is a goal of a school or center, planning in advance to collect documentation that might become part of children's assessment portfolios saves time. The anticipatory planning process outlined in Chapter 7 provides a way to anticipate where required curriculum and achievement of standards might occur in project work. As part of the ceiling work done at the beginning of the project, teachers can plan to include the proper methods of documentation. By anticipating documentation for assessment, materials and equipment can be ready and accessible.

The processing of documentation can also be prioritized according to its use. A teacher who was in an especially challenging teaching situation was heard to say that she could not do projects because she did not have time to spend on "those displays." This is a misunderstanding of the role of documentation in project work. Documentation takes many forms—from raw documentation, such as untranscribed tapes and children's work fresh off the easel, to polished display boards and transcripts. Teachers can save time if they approach the use of documentation as a distilling process, as discussed in *Windows on Learning* (Helm et al., 1998), and make decisions about how much time to spend on the different pieces of documentation they collect. For example, documentation for the purpose of guiding instruction is gathered and used to inform teaching during the progress of the project. Some of this documentation might be annotated for portfolios or for assessment; some might be selected without annotations or additional preparation for display within the classroom; some may be matted for display outside the classroom; some very special documentation might be selected for sharing and discussing with colleagues during staff development meetings; and some may be carefully and professionally prepared to share outside of the school in public places such as libraries, hospitals, or field-site locations.

Although documentation greatly increases the value of project work, it is difficult to provide guidance as to how much is necessary for teachers facing challenges. When a teacher has to decide whether to spend time after school transcribing a tape of a dialogue or searching for a library book on that specific aspect of the topic that might open Jamal's eyes to the value of books and reading, there are no rules that can be applied.

Documentation has enormous power. We have seen it reach parents and families in ways unlike any other teaching method. We have seen parents moved to tears as documentation revealed the growth in knowledge and skills of their children. When administrators see how children are learning and applying academic skills, such as this kindergarten's writing numbers in thousands (see Figure 8.2), they see the value of project work

Figure 8.2 During the Garage Project field-site visit, Erik asked how much a new car costs. He remembered the answer—$15,000 to $40,000—and made a price list for the class's garage construction.

and other engaged learning experiences. We have seen administrators reallocate resources and develop support systems based on a growing understanding of this way of learning.

Just as there is no one right way to do projects with children, there is no one way to approach documentation. How much documentation is processed and shared and how much time is spent on documentation will have to be determined by the philosophy of the program, the value the teacher places upon documentation, and the administrative support given to the documentation process. It is all a journey.

Documentation and assessment can add significantly to the effectiveness of project work in schools and centers where teachers are facing challenges. There are many reasons to make documentation (including assessment) an important part of the project process. The purpose of project work is not to produce impressive documentation, however; the goal is to help children learn and enable teachers to become better at helping them do it.

REFERENCES

Beneke, S. (1998). *Rearview mirror: Reflections on a preschool car project.* Champaign, IL: ERIC Clearinghouse on Elementary and Early Childhood Education.

Chard, S. (1998). *The project approach: Making curriculum come alive* (Bk. 1). New York: Scholastic, Inc.

Dahlberg, G., Moss, P., & Pence, A. R. (1999). *Beyond quality in early childhood education and care: Postmodern perspectives.* London: Taylor & Francis.

Dichtelmiller, M. L., Jablon, J. R., Dorfman, A. B., Marsden, D. B., & Meisels, S. J. (1997). *Work sampling in the classroom: A teacher's manual.* Ann Arbor, MI: Rebus Planning Associates.

Gardner, H. (1993). *Frames of the mind.* New York: Basic Books.

Gronlund, G., & Engel, B. (2001). *Focused portfolios: A complete assessment for the young child.* Saint Paul, MN: Redleaf Press.

Gullo, D. F. (1994). *Understanding assessment and evaluation in early childhood education.* New York: Teachers College Press.

Helm, J. H., Beneke, S., & Steinheimer, K. (1998). *Windows on learning: Documenting young children's work.* New York: Teachers College Press.

Helm, J. H., & Katz, L. G. (2001). *Young investigators: The project approach in the early years.* New York: Teachers College Press.

Katz, L. G., & Chard, S. C. (1989). *Engaging children's minds: The project approach.* Greenwich, CT: Ablex.

Meisels, S. J. (1993). Remaking classroom assessment with the work sampling system. *Young Children, 48*(5), 34–40.

Meisels, S. J. (1995). *Performance assessment in early childhood education: The work sampling system. Eric digest.* Urbana, IL: ERIC Clearinghouse on Elementary and Early Childhood Education.

Meisels, S. J., Bickel, D. D., Nicholson, J., Xue, Y., & Atkins-Burnett, S. (2001). Trusting teachers' judgments: A validity study of a curriculum-embedded performance assessment in kindergarten to grade 3. *American Educational Research Journal, 38*(1), 73–95.

Rinaldi, C. (2001). Documentation and assessment: What is the relationship? In C. Giudici, C. Rinaldi, & M. Krechevsky (Eds.), *Making learning visible: Children as individual and group learners* (pp. 78–89). Reggio Emilia, Italy: Reggio Children.

CHAPTER 9

Future Challenges: Concluding Thoughts

Judy Harris Helm

PRINCIPLES FOR THE DISCOVERY OF NEW KNOWLEDGE

In a hospital waiting room one day, I was browsing through a copy of *Science* magazine, a publication for scientific researchers, when I came across an editorial by two research physicians, David Paydarfar and William J. Schwartz.[1] They shared their ideas about the processes of creating new knowledge by "asking the right question, pursuing the unknown, making discoveries" and about "boosting the rate and magnitude of discoveries" (Paydarfar & Schwartz, 2001, p. 13). Their analysis resulted in an "algorithm for discovery"—five simple principles for creating new knowledge.

What struck me was the similarity between their principles, which I quote below, and the experiences we advocate for young children when they are engaged in project work.

1. Slow down to explore. Discovery is facilitated by an unhurried attitude. We favor a relaxed yet attentive and prepared state of mind that is free of the checklists, deadlines, and other exigencies of the workday schedule. (p. 13)

In the project approach, teachers are encouraged to follow, support, and extend children's interest for as long as they remain reasonably curious about the topic and are developing more questions. Instead of learning about a particular piece of information for a week (much of it "presented" by the teacher), then moving on to the next piece, children are encouraged to come up with a list of further questions and then proceed to find the answers. Projects evolve as the children progress and their questions become more focused and in depth. Projects often last four to six weeks or even longer.

2. Read, but not too much. It is important to master what others have already written. Published works are the forum for scientific discourse and embody the accumulated experience of the research community. But the influence of experts can be powerful and might quash a nascent idea before it can take root. (p. 13)

We advocate that young children read books and listen to stories related to the topic under investigation to develop background knowledge and build vocabulary; but then we encourage them to engage in firsthand exploration as a way of helping them to learn that they can often find answers to their questions directly, without using books. They learn that knowledge is not only what someone else has already said or done and that they can construct their own ideas. Literacy skills then become valuable tools for thinking, checking their thinking with that of others, and representing their findings with words that they either write or dictate to someone else who can write for them. In these ways, children create books that represent the process by which they learned about the topic.

3. Pursue quality for its own sake. Time spent refining methods and design is almost always rewarded. Rigorous attention

---

Excerpts with permission from Paydarfar, D., & Schwartz, W. J. (2001). "An algorithm for discovery." *Science 292*, 13. Printed with permission of the American Association for the Advancement of Science.

[1]David Paydarfar and William J. Schwartz are in the Department of Neurology, University of Massachusetts Medical School. Their article was adapted from lectures given at the University of North Carolina and the University of California.

to such details helps to avert the premature rejection or acceptance of hypotheses. Sometimes, in the process of perfecting one's approach, unexpected discoveries can be made. (p. 13)

During good project work children are encouraged to review their own work and evaluate their own thinking. For example, we encourage children to sketch and draw relevant objects from observations. We then encourage them to look at the object again redraw it as they learn more about it. Throughout the project, the teacher collects children's successive attempts at drawing or constructing and encourages them to examine the sequence and to talk about additions and changes to each attempt. The teacher also engages the children in discussions of how the representations changed, what they did differently or wanted to do better, and what they think remains to be learned. Children are encouraged to help each other through advice and suggestions on what to add to their representations or how they might refine their questions.

4. Look at the raw data. There is no substitute for viewing the data at first hand. Take a seat at the bedside and interview the patient yourself; watch the oscilloscope trace; inspect the gel while still wet. (p. 13)

We encourage children to develop the habit of gathering data by using interviews, surveys, and tally sheets to record their observations (even three-year-olds can do tally sheets). In other words, projects provide contexts in which young children develop the disposition to seek information for themselves and then record and process this new information. For example, while studying farm machinery, children found out how many wheels each machine had by counting them and making tally graphs.

5. Cultivate smart friends. Sharing with a buddy can sharpen critical thinking and spark new insights. (p. 13)

Projects are collaborative experiences—usually children work in groups based on their interests. They learn to work together toward a goal and to appreciate the unique gifts of each child in their class.

OUR NATION'S CHALLENGES

As the events of September 11, 2001, reminded us, predicting the future is difficult, if not impossible. Our current understanding of what our nation and its children will face in the future is limited. We cannot predict what new knowledge and discoveries will be needed in medicine, environmental science, education, economics, or social relations. We do know, however, that those who will be responsible for these new discoveries are in our classrooms today, and their knowledge, skills, and dispositions largely will be determined by how well their teachers overcome the challenges they face.

When we observe the teachers whose projects fill this book—who are facing the challenges of teaching today—we see the impact they have on the development of not only their student's knowledge and skills but also their curiosity and intellectual dispositions. As Lilian Katz explained in chapter 2, "what teachers do with children all day" can build a solid foundation for the intellectual work our society will need in the future. Teachers can have an enormous impact on the capability of today's children to face the challenges of tomorrow.

As Paydarfar and Schwartz (2001) hope that their "essay can serve as an inspiration for reclaiming the process of discovery and making it a part of the daily routine" (p. 13), we hope that teachers will do good project work with children, maximizing its impact by using our suggested practical strategies for overcoming challenges. It is in the best interest of this nation that all children, regardless of what is happening in their lives today, develop both the academic skills and intellectual dispositions necessary to meet the challenges of the future.

REFERENCE

Paydarfar, D., & Schwartz, W. J. (2001). Algorithm for discovery. *Science 292*(5514), 13.

Frequently Asked Questions and Practical Advice

While helping teachers learn how to use project work to meet the challenges discussed in this book, we have encountered many questions. At the same time, we have found that the most helpful and practical advice for implementation of the project approach comes from those in the field actually doing project work. What follows are some of the questions most frequently asked of the teachers and administrators who contributed to this book along with information they felt would be beneficial for other early childhood teachers facing the challenges discussed in this book.

I know parent involvement is helpful for meeting these challenges, but how can I make it happen in my program?

Jean Lang

Parent involvement is especially helpful in meeting the challenges discussed in this book. Yet, these same challenges can make involving parents more difficult. Establishing trust can be more challenging when a teacher is a different race, culture, or socioeconomic class than parents. Parents' jobs may leave little time for school activities, and parents with limited financial resources may be unaware that they have other opportunities to share with schools. Parents of second-language learners, often non-native English speakers themselves, may have difficulty communicating with their child's teachers, and parents from minority cultures may not feel comfortable in the school environment. Parents of children with special needs may see the school as a source of stress. All of these parents have much to contribute, and teachers may need to make particular efforts to tap into those resources.

Honor and Value Family Culture and Religion

Teachers must make special efforts to be sensitive to other cultures, values, and attitudes; be aware of all cultural groups within their classrooms and schools; learn about the customs and holidays of each family's culture; utilize support staff, such as translators and family support staff, whenever needed; prepare translated materials to be distributed with English materials; and use translators for conferences, meetings, and site visits.

Build Rapport Through Home Visits

Home visits are a good way to begin a working relationship with families. Teachers must be flexible about the meeting time, place, and day. Some families prefer to meet at a restaurant, place of business, or school rather than their homes, and parents' work schedules may necessitate meeting after school hours. After teachers establish trust and a bond with the family, a follow-up visit to their home may be possible. During the initial home visit, I like to give parents a copy of my classroom handbook, which explains the routines and procedures of my classroom and our district program. This information helps families understand the system, and the handbook is a source of information for families who might be hesitant to ask questions in person.

Home visits provide an excellent opportunity to introduce the project approach to families; teachers may want to take along a handout explaining the project approach and mention past classroom projects. *Young Investigators* (Helm & Katz, 2001) contains an excellent handout that explains the project approach.

Get Families into the Classroom

Teachers should clearly indicate to parents that they have an open-door policy, and that parents and families may visit at any time without an appointment. This deepens trust and lets families stop by for a few minutes in a busy schedule to observe a project study in process. At the end of a project, many families are eager to attend culminating activities that display the children's work.

Communicate What Is Going on in the Classroom

Once school has started, teachers can keep families informed through newsletters, phone calls, and pictures. I include photos and direct quotes from children in newsletters and have adopted a practice called Daily Journals—daily newsletters that document one or two activities taking place in the classroom. I also use digital photos and scanned samples of children's work to illustrate one significant activity from both my morning and afternoon group twice a week. Project work lends itself to a daily journal and lets teachers document significant events in time.

Encourage Volunteering

Teachers need to communicate to parents specific ways they can help. If teachers let families know what materials or needs the children have, they often become involved in the project. All families have resources, skills, and strengths. It is very important that teachers not make assumptions about those strengths and resources. Parents can be invited into the classroom to share hobbies, traditions, interests, and resources, which often leads to new interests and even projects to investigate. Teachers may find it easier to begin by inviting families whose children have been in their class in previous years, so a relationship has already been developed

Project study offers many opportunities to increase parental involvement and for families to interact in a meaningful way with other families and the school. Teachers who capitalize on the skills, knowledge, and resources of families deepen the bond between child, teachers, families, and their communities.

How do I organize my classroom so that I can meet standards and accomplish required curriculum?

Jean Thieman

Curriculum can include both activities designed by the teacher and project work. When doing project work,

I review district curriculum goals and state standards so I can integrate them into the project. I am careful to make sure the topic is consistent with the curriculum and extensive enough to encompass many of the goals. Then I develop a teacher web, which demonstrates the possible directions for the project. I add the domains, curriculum goals, and state standards that can be implemented. These coordinate with the Work Sampling System, our school's assessment tool.

Curriculum Integration in Phase I

During the initial phase of a project, I work with small, flexible groups of children and provide an environment for exploration where they develop the project direction and questions. For example, during our initial study of water, described in Chapter 4, the children actively investigated various characteristics of water at the water table and through teacher-guided experiments in floating/sinking, water pressure, and evaporation/condensation. The students practiced scientific thinking by observing, predicting or hypothesizing, and comparing aspects of the experiments. As a part of the evaporation/condensation experiment, the children wrote daily journal entries of what was happening to their water-in-a-bag, thereby incorporating writing goals as well as scientific thinking.

If possible, we make a site visit to further stimulate interest and questions and incorporate observational skills and vocabulary development. In the Water to River Project, one group used the encyclopedia, classroom books, and pamphlets as sources of information and to study diagrams of fish and then presented their information and bass model to the class.

Curriculum Integration in Phase II

In Phase II, students delve into their particular interest. Much of the research, construction, and creating takes place during center or choice time. In this way we incorporate required curriculum into the project, making the best use of our school time. The students help plan some of the centers, while the teacher prepares others based on the initial planning web and the needs of the students. Some of the learning centers are set up for investigations or independent choice with ownership by the children. Others are developed for the teaching team, so notes can be taken, observations made, and lessons taught. Often, two of the centers relate to language and literacy, such as computer research, vocabulary development, creative writing, or book making. Others involve math, science, and art. The paint center and construction areas allow for natural integration of fine arts goals. The students' paintings and building activities often reflect their investigations. They write or dictate about their paintings and draw their constructions. In the quiet area, we always have a supply of books and tapes about the topic. This encourages children to practice reading and listening skills. During center time, the students make their own work choices, though the degree of choice may vary at times. Some children may return to the same learning center for several days to complete some aspect of the project, while others may spend less time in that area. This helps children develop persistence and focus on achievement of a goal, both of which are personal-social goals for our children.

Following center time, we gather to discuss our progress, clarify ideas, share and record information or problems, and evaluate what we have accomplished. These discussions allow us to reflect and be open about our strengths and mistakes and to use problem-solving skills to determine the next steps. This gives guidance and structure to our plan and helps prepare us for the following day. The remainder of our day is spent with the regular curriculum, though some of our choice and shared reading activities may relate to the project.

Curriculum Integration in Phase III

Finally, we determine how we will culminate or share our knowledge about the project. This, too, is done during discussion and center time. In the Water to River Project, for example, the class discussed how we could combine our focus on saving water and keeping it clean with our interest in fish. They concluded that a display near the school entry would be easily noticed. To draw the attention of a wider audience, the girls and boys wanted to share many of their paintings, letters to other classrooms emphasizing saving water, writings, and posters. During center time, individuals and groups selected the best examples to display, using reading and language skills. One group painted a river backdrop of dirty water and one of clean water. Another decided on the title of the display and made the letters for it. Finally, a small group worked with the teachers to hang the display in two distinct parts: a clean river with its growth and balance and a dirty river with little growth or balance of nature.

As we discussed and revisited our information, I was able to observe, take notes, and collect samples of each child's project work to assess individual development and progress. Some of the collected work was spontaneous—paintings, writings, dramatic play, or constructions that came directly from the child's reactions to lessons, investigations, readings, discussions, and site visits. Other work may be based on the child's observations or reflections of specific experiments or the development and interpretation of graphs or maps.

Each year I learn more about projects and what children can accomplish through them. Project work involves trial-and-error and practice to develop strategies and techniques that work for individual teaching styles. More and more, I recognize the value of observing students and probing their responses. Observing provides necessary information for making decisions about when and how to intervene with children to better meet their needs and extend their thinking in the curriculum areas. When I use information about the children's interests, I am able to provide meaningful practice of academic skills that children are intrinsically motivated to do. Additionally, as I step back, the children rely more on each other as teachers and resources. Finally, through projects, teaching the curriculum becomes more personally and intellectually satisfying to me. I model intellectual development and enthusiasm for learning for my children. The key to success is to make the project approach work for you.

Is technology helpful to teachers facing these challenges? If it is, what kind of technology should a school or center provide for project work?

Char Ward and Sharon Doubet

Basic Technology That Is Useful for Projects

When teachers facilitate projects, they can use computers, color printers, digital cameras, camcorders, VCRs and monitors, scanners, tape recorders, overhead projectors, and CD players. One teacher we know uses a scan converter hooked to a TV monitor to show pictures related to projects. Another teacher takes a digital camera and camcorder on all class excursions to document learning for assessment purposes and allow the class to revisit experiences. These technology tools are integrated into all parts of the day as a way to gain and share information, investigate, and revisit the children's field experiences.

Specific Software to Support Project Work

Technology can support all facets of daily project work. A visual organization program, such as Kidspiration by Inspiration Software, facilitates the development of the teacher anticipatory planning web using both words and pictures. Kidspiration can also be used as a tool to create a web describing the children's prior knowledge of a topic, what children want to know about the topic, and what they learn throughout the project. Multimedia slide shows of project work are easily created with programs such as Kids Pix Studio Deluxe by Riverdeep. Hyperstudio by Knowledge

Adventure also can be used to prepare a multimedia documentation of project work, including narration with the children's voices. Multimedia technology supports the growth of receptive and expressive language in classrooms.

Gaining Knowledge in the Area of Technology

Usually early childhood personnel must develop their own expertise or support for technology, although sometimes a program will also nourish the development of a staff member interested in technology. It is helpful if the quest for knowledge about technology is viewed as the teacher's own project. What do we know? What do we want to know? What resources are available? Who are the experts? When teachers begin to develop their own dispositions and skills with respect to computers, printers, scanners, cameras, and software, they can begin to make wise decisions in regard to their often limited resources.

Accessing Funds to Support Technology

Often budgets do not include funds for technology for early childhood education, or an administration does not understand the extent to which technology can support young children's work. When teachers increase their knowledge about technology, it is possible to educate those who make budget decisions. It is helpful to be able to show how others use technology in project work. Sometimes a parents' group will help obtain a classroom computer and printer, or local businesses may have special rates on discontinued printers, digital cameras, scanners, and the like, if teachers take the time to ask.

Example of Integration of Technology in a Project

In a project on trains in an early childhood classroom, the following integration of technology occurred:

Phase I. Children became interested in the topic of trains through a CD-ROM story, *Just Me and My Mom* (Mayer, 1990). The teacher used a software program to make an anticipatory planning web. The Internet was used to find community resources, possible field sites, and expert visitors. The teacher made a computer version of the web showing what the children knew and what they wanted to know. Children used additional CD-ROMs to learn more about trains.

Phase II. A digital camera and camcorder were used to record a trip to the train depot. Observational sketches were scanned and made into books. A TV and VCR were used to revisit the field-site visit and do Time 2

sketches. Children consulted the photos and video during construction of a model train. A new web was created about what they had learned about trains.

Phase III. A software program was used to create a slide show of the train project. A word processing program enabled the children to help create invitations to the culminating event. Children's work (products, observations, audio and video tapes) were incorporated into each child's portfolio, and the teacher used a computerized reporting program to inform parents of the knowledge, skills, and dispositions observed during the project.

Is Internet access helpful for project work? How might a teacher use the Internet in dealing with these challenges?

Dianne Rothenberg

Access to the Internet can help teachers use the project approach to meet the challenges facing today's schools. The Internet can be used as a tool to communicate about the project approach with other teachers, a source of information on the project approach itself, and a source of reference or additional topical information for implementing the project approach.

Online Communication

The most important Internet resource for project work is *other knowledgeable teachers*, including educators and experts experienced in the project approach. Online communication—particularly e-mail—can facilitate one-to-one communication in an informal context. Access to the online world can reduce the isolation of a teacher who may be the only one in his or her school using the project approach or who is trying the project approach for the first time.

Although many listservs—such as REGGIO-L@ listserv.cso.uiuc.edu or ECENET-L@listserv.cso.uiuc. edu—may occasionally include discussions of project work, PROJECTS-L@listserv.cso.uiuc.edu is devoted entirely to discussion of projects in the classroom. Complete information about subscribing to PROJECTS-L (subscriptions are free) is located at http://ericeece.org/listserv/projec-l.html.

Teachers use PROJECTS-L and other listservs related to the project approach to

- Elicit the help of colleagues in brainstorming about a problem encountered during the implementation of a project
- Confer with other teachers facing the same challenges
- Find out how children with special needs can become involved in projects

- Discuss ideas for displaying and documenting children's work
- Seek help in finding project-related resources
- Share with colleagues success stories about how the project approach has helped to meet challenges

Belonging to a listserv can expand a teacher's network of peers to an international community of learners who are interested in and knowledgeable about either the project approach generally or issues associated with specific challenges, such as responding to children's special needs or helping children learn a second language. Listservs can provide a comfortable, nonthreatening context for asking questions about project work and discussing concerns about children's progress. The archives of PROJECTS-L's discussions are available at http://askeric.org/Virtual/Listserv_Archives/PROJECTS-L.shtml and searchable by topic or the name of any person contributing a message to the ongoing discussions.

Web sites that focus on implementation of the project approach are a second kind of resource for teachers undertaking project work. In addition to providing guidance for teachers, these web sites can be a source of information to share with parents, school boards, and community members.

ERIC/EECE maintains several high-quality links to project approach web sites at http://ericeece.org/project.html. The ERIC database offers access to journal articles, reports, guides, and books written on the project approach. To search ERIC on the Internet, users can go to AskERIC at http://www.askeric.org.

Using the Web to Help Move Young Children Toward Literacy

Children's observations of how adults find and use facts and nonfiction information can provide good examples of the importance adults place on literacy. The need for information in context, such as in the course of an investigation, offers teachers a chance to increase a child's interest in text and the development of reading by modeling use of encyclopedias, other reference books, and the Internet to solve real problems.

In most preschool and elementary school classrooms, children are encouraged to use books, encyclopedias, and other reference works to find information about the objects they are studying. All too often, however, classrooms, school library media centers, and public libraries may need to augment on-site collections with additional recently published, high-quality topical information.

Teachers can use the Internet to find information on topics that are likely to be investigated in their class using search engines such as AltaVista (http://altavista.digital.com/) or Google (http://www.google.com). This process might begin after a concept web has been produced.

Some web sites contain basic reference tools, such as up-to-date encyclopedias, that may not be available in every child's center, preschool, or elementary school classroom. The following sites offer access to dictionaries and encyclopedias and other basic reference sources:

- Internet Public Library: http://www.ipl.org/ref/RR/
- Encyclopedia.Com: http://www.encyclopedia.com/
- Encyberpedia: The Living Encyclopedia: http://www.encyberpedia.com/eindex.htm

In addition to general works, the Internet can provide access to some specialized and useful collections of information for projects. For example, students engaged in a project at a nearby pond may need supporting information to help them classify the frogs in the pond or identify their sounds (try the Froggy Page at http://www.frogsonice.com/froggy/). They can also find more specific information on Illinois frogs at Illinois Frog and Toad Facts (http://dnr.state.il.us/lands/education/frog/), a page maintained by the Illinois Department of Natural Resources.

Similarly, students interested in doing a project on birds can start with the Texas Parks and Wildlife web site's "A Children's Guide to Bird Watching" at http://www.tpwd.state.tx.us/adv/birding/beginbird/kidbird.htm and then move on to http://home.xnet.com/~ugeiser/Birds/Birding.html to learn more.

In addition to providing text, web sites may use a combination of sounds, graphic images, diagrams, and animation, which engage emerging readers. Even when it is not feasible for children to use the Internet themselves in the classroom, the web can be a source of photos, diagrams, and sketches that teachers can use to support project work.

When meeting challenges with projects, what documentation should I share with the community?

Amanda Helm

Project documentation is most often thought of as a way for teachers to understand children's learning and improve teaching. However, sharing project documentation can be a way to communicate children's accomplishments, build support for the school, and foster understanding of the project approach. This sharing can involve parents in their child's education and build a positive image of the child as a learner, both of which help meet the challenges discussed in this book.

There is so much to share about a project that it can be hard to know where to start or what to include. Sometimes the children decide what to share during Phase III. In many situations, however, the main purpose of sharing project documentation is to communicate meaningfully with adult audiences.

Project documentation is more effective when it is used to support or explain a point. Teachers can use documentation to prove points they want to make rather than simply reporting that the project happened. For example, it might be more beneficial to show how children are meeting the first-grade reading goals through project work rather than just to describe what happened in Phase II of the project. When deciding what to share, consider these two keys to effective communication:

- Tight focus
- Relevant message

Tight Focus

It is not possible to share everything! Documentation can be more effective when the teacher is realistic about what the audience can grasp quickly with minimal attention. Remember that people may be reading the display in passing or skimming the article.

Teachers may want to limit themselves to one to three main points (less for displays, more for written documents such as newsletters). *Almost* everything said should relate to those points, preferably by providing details and examples to "prove" them.

Almost!? There are probably other, relational messages that teachers want to communicate, such as showing their credibility or liking and appreciation of the audience. These messages are the exception—they are nice to communicate as long as they do not distract from the display's main point. If these goals are particularly important, consider them as unstated main points including in the one to three maximum. For example, possible main points for a display to be shown to a business where a class took a field trip might be

1. The project approach teaches children creative problem solving
2. Your employees really helped our kids learn. Thank you!

Point 2 might not be explicitly stated on the display, which mainly would relate to creative problem solving, but the photos and other documentation would emphasize the employees' role.

One way to ensure that the display focuses on one to three main points is for teachers to write out the points (including unstated ones) on a piece of paper and put the paper where it can be seen while working. The main points can be supplemented with photos, anecdotes about children's work, children's sketches and tallies, and so forth. Time 1 and Time 2 drawings displayed side-by-side can be especially convincing. Less is more—a few large photos or drawings will be more eye catching and memorable than many small ones.

Relevant Message

Teachers must remember to design displays to say what the audience needs to hear, not what teachers want to say. What teachers say should have an obvious personal impact on the audience. If it is not immediately obvious why the documentation is important, explain why as part of the display, article, or web page. Ideally, the points teachers choose to convey will also help them get important issues across to the audience.

Questions to Consider When Deciding What to Say

Who is the audience? Parents? Community members? School board? The primary audience probably is not other teachers, so the audience might not have the same interests as the teacher creating the documentation.

What is the audience looking for? Do they want or need something specific from this communication? Will they be looking at the documentation with questions in mind? If so, be sure to provide answers to those questions.

Teachers also should consider how they want the audience to respond. "After reading my documentation display, the school board members will...." If teachers want the audience members to take action, it should be stated explicitly ("Businesses can help by....") To change people's thinking, documentation should act as a persuasive argument with supporting information. Is this a one-time communication or part of a series? Is there an opportunity to build knowledge over time or to repeat important messages? If so, it would probably be best to present bite-size pieces of information each time. For example, math goals could be emphasized for one project and literacy goals for another, instead of trying to show all the ways that one project helps meet standards.

Other factors teachers should keep in mind are what do audience members already know; what do audience members think they know; how can their misconceptions be corrected; and what background information will they need. If teachers have to start from the beginning because the audience has little knowledge of the project approach, there are limits to what they can hope to communicate.

When planning to use one display or another communication piece for several audiences, consider if the audiences share enough needs in common that it makes sense to combine them. It might be better to make a display that can easily change to meet different audiences' needs.

As an administrator, I want to help my teachers use the project approach. What is my role in getting projects going in my school? How can I support teachers?

Cathy Wiggers and Maxine Wortham

Integrating the curriculum and providing opportunities for problem solving and engaged learning through the project approach takes time, planning, and preparation. The administrator serves as the visionary, instructional leader, and resource provider in the implementation of projects.

As the keeper of the vision and mission of the school, it is essential that administrators actively communicate their support of the project approach. The administrative leader is the role model who displays behaviors that reinforce the values of the school. If teachers perceive a lack of administrative support for the project approach, they will be discouraged from implementing it. If parents or school board or community members perceive lukewarm support from authoritative administrators, it may fuel doubts about the validity of engaged learning approaches that differ from traditional "seatwork." Communicating support can be especially important if only a few teachers in a school are using the project approach.

Create a Vision of a Project School

The administrator plays a critical role in communicating to both school and community audiences that the project approach is valid and important. In enacting this role, administrators should keep these points in mind:

1. Provide central, visible display areas within the school where children are able to share their learning with others through drawings, photographs, murals, and three-dimensional representations.
2. Encourage teachers to communicate their knowledge and experiences with the broader community. Avenues for sharing might include local, state, and national educational conferences. Museums, banks, or other places of business may display the children's work for a period of time. The children's field

site may make a good display site. A sharing night in the spring is a good opportunity for other programs or schools in the surrounding area to come together to display projects and talk with one another about their work.
3. Encourage parents to be present in the school and classrooms as observers and volunteers.
4. Use "project monthly reports" within the school to enhance communication between staff members and the principal/director. Teachers record the topic, the current phase of the project, the activities the class is involved in, and field-site visit information. This communication keeps the administrator informed of the project's progress, the need for additional support when necessary, and the opportunity to give feedback if desired by the teacher or administrator.
5. Visit classrooms to see the progress of the projects the children are working on and listen to them talk about their work. See how children learn by letting them show what they are doing and thinking.

Help Teachers Learn the Project Approach

Learning to do projects with young children is a challenge. To be successful in using the project approach, teachers need the support of their administrators. Principals/directors can help teachers learn about project work in the following ways:

- Plan training time for all teachers and administrators to become grounded in using the project approach. Training can take place in a variety of ways; however, it takes approximately two to three days of training to feel confident enough to embark upon and complete a project for the first time. Two full days of training with a follow-up day one month later is an ideal way to help teachers begin project work. If this schedule is not possible, five evenings over the course of two months may be adequate; follow-up training is advisable.
- Provide time to develop projects through team planning, thereby making the curriculum come alive. Schedule time for teachers to come together for a one- to two-hour block of time each week for developing projects and planning curriculum.
- Recognize that communication is the key to having a collaborative climate in the school. Project sharing groups can meet over coffee in the morning or during lunch on Friday. The groups can meet every few weeks to talk about their classes' projects. Informal discussions allow for progress to be shared or problem solving to take place as needed. Teachers can help one another determine the best places for a particular field experience, where to find an expert to visit the classroom, or how to support children in a

certain way to help them carry out their work. It is important for the principal/director to take part in these groups as a supportive listener and problem solver.

Provide Resources and Be Flexible

Administrators must support a problem-solving classroom, allowing the teacher to alter the environment and provide resources and materials appropriate for engaging in an in-depth study. Teachers must give up some control over classroom activities and learn to be flexible—adjusting lesson plans to follow children's areas of interest and changing activity plans quickly to allow children to implement their own plans and ideas. Often teachers need to change plans in a day or two. For teachers to achieve this level of flexibility, they need to be supported by a flexible school system, which includes these characteristics:

- The learners in the classroom, both teachers and children, must be given the autonomy to work together through projects and topics of study that excite and challenge children in appropriate ways. It may be difficult, if not impossible, for teachers to follow rigidly controlled curricula while following the lead of young investigators through a project. At least part of the school day must be available for teachers to structure as is appropriate for their individual classrooms.
- Allow flexibility in scheduling to provide extended work times for in-depth study of the topic. Long blocks of work time without interruptions are needed so that content areas can be integrated into the project work based on the interests of the children. Sometimes the schedule may need to be altered according to heightened interest, needs of the children, and their progress on the project.
- Provide systems that allow teachers to obtain supplies quickly as the project evolves. Teachers will be able to help children carry out their project work with many donated materials that are easy to find. For occasions when something does need to be purchased with funds from the classroom/program/school budget, it is helpful for teachers to be able to get approval and purchase the items in a timely manner. This process can be expedited by reimbursing the teacher for the purchases or having a school charge account at a store such as Wal-Mart.
- Allow field trips to be planned and taken at key times in investigations to further learning and progress in the study. For learning to be encouraged and not hindered, the timing of field work during a project can be crucial. Approval of field trips within a few

days is helpful. It is important for the teacher to visit the site ahead of time to work out the logistics of group work at the site and to prepare the experts at the site for their role in teaching/sharing with the children. It works best if field trips are scheduled as needed rather than having a preset schedule of one field trip per month or quarter.

How can I help preservice teachers learn about the project approach so they will be able to use it to meet challenges when they begin to teach?

Sallee Beneke

Todays's preservice teachers are likely to face a variety of challenges in their future classrooms. There is no single way to provide training in the project approach to preservice students or to assure that they will be equipped to implement the approach in diverse settings, which can include urban, rural, part-day, child care, preschool, inclusive, or linguistically diverse schools and centers. Firsthand experiences can be provided for students in schools and centers where project work is used. Instructors can also add activities related to projects to their existing courses or develop a new course on the project approach.

Activities Added to Existing Courses

Guest Experts. Whenever possible, it is beneficial to give students the opportunity to hear about using the project approach from teachers who are using it in the field. Classroom practitioners can be invited to visit, share examples from their experiences, and answer questions. Discussion with practicing teachers over the Internet, videotape recordings of teachers, or written descriptions help students see the potential of this approach to benefit children with diverse backgrounds and needs.

Scenarios. A very helpful resource in teaching students to think about and understand the flexible, emergent nature of the project approach can be scenarios of projects in process that are written by the instructor. These scenarios are likely to help students recognize the need for cross-cultural competency. They are especially effective when they include obstacles created by the challenges of including children with special needs, implementing standards while teaching in a child-sensitive manner, incorporating language and literacy skills, engaging children from at-risk backgrounds, and involving parents in classroom activities. Discussions that come out of such scenarios help future teachers recognize their own biases, identify areas where they need further professional development, and encourage their confidence that the project approach can be used effectively in a wide variety of classroom situations.

Learning from the Work of Others. During the course, students can be given opportunities to look at the project work of other teachers. By looking at examples of real projects, students can learn to identify the events that commonly take place during each of the three phases of a project and to recognize the ways that practicing teachers have supported children in their investigations. Projects can be viewed at the ERIC-EECE web site (http://ericeece.org/project.html). One-page summaries of projects are also available online in the *Project Approach Catalog 1 & 2* (http://ericeece.org). Students can take an in-depth look at projects through the Fire Truck Project, documented in *Young Investigators* (Helm & Katz, 2001); the Mail Project, documented in *Windows on Learning* (Helm, Beneke, & Steinheimer, 1998); and the Car Project, documented in *Rearview Mirror: Reflections on a Preschool Car Project* (Beneke, 1998).

Courses Focused on the Project

Adding a course on the project approach to the early childhood education curriculum can introduce preservice students to both the theory and practice of the project approach and documentation. During the course, small groups of students can conduct an in-depth project and then prepare a panel to document the story of their project and the growth in their understanding about the value of this approach to teaching. This experience helps form personal notions of what constitutes a project and helps students develop an appreciation for teamwork and collaboration. Many students have preconceived definitions for the word *project*. They often think of a project as a defined task. Conducting their own project helps them to construct new meaning for the word *project* and to develop an understanding of how curriculum can emerge from children's interests.

REFERENCES

Beneke, S. (1998). *Rearview mirror: Reflections on a preschool car project.* Champaign, IL: ERIC Clearinghouse on Elementary and Early Childhood Education.

Helm, J. H., Beneke, S., & Steinheimer, K. (1998). *Windows on learning: Documenting young children's work.* New York: Teachers College Press.

Helm, J. H., & Katz, L. G. (2001). *Young investigators: The project approach in the early years.* New York: Teachers College Press.

Mayer, Mercer. (1990). *Just me and my mom* [Computer software]. Roxbury, CT: Big Tuna Media.

Recommended Resources

LEARNING TO USE THE PROJECT APPROACH

These books and resources provide information on the project process and how to use the project approach in classrooms.

Katz, Lilian G., & Helm, Judy Harris. (2001). *Young Investigators: The Project Approach in the Early Years.* Early Childhood Education Series. Available from Teachers College Press, P.O. Box 20, Williston, VT 05495-0020. 145pp.

Katz and Harris have provided a step-by-step guide for doing projects with children who are not yet proficient at reading and writing. Each phase is described in detail with practical advice from teachers using the project approach in classrooms for toddlers through first grade. A planning journal at the end of the book guides teachers who are new to project work through the project process with checklists and reflection questions. The journal also organizes documentation for those teachers more experienced with project work. The Fire Truck Project, which took place in a preschool classroom with children with special needs, is described in detail. An accompanying video, *A Children's Journey: The Fire Truck Project*, enables viewers to see the children involved in the project and hear the teacher describe the process of the project. The video is also available from Teachers College Press.

Katz, Lilian G., & Chard, Sylvia C. (2000). *Engaging Children's Minds: The Project Approach* (2nd ed.). Available from Ablex Publishing Corp., P.O. Box 811, Stamford, CT 06904-0811. 215pp.

This latest edition of the classic description of the project approach presents the theoretical base of the approach and suggests ways to apply it in elementary school classrooms. Each phase of project work is discussed with examples.

Chard, Sylvia C. (1998). *Project Approach: Developing the Basic Framework, Practical Guide 1* and *Project Approach: Developing Curriculum with Children, Practical Guide 2.* Available from Scholastic, Inc., 555 Broadway, New York, NY 10012. 64pp.

These guides are especially helpful for teachers of children who are old enough to independently use reading and writing as learning tools. They present many classroom ideas to support and integrate curriculum activities into project work. The three phases of project work are described fully and teacher and student roles are discussed.

Early Childhood Research and Practice. Lilian G. Katz, Editor; Dianne Rothenberg, Associate Editor; an Internet journal on the development, care, and education of young children located at http://ecrp.uiuc.edu/.

This online journal is published in the fall and spring and regularly features project work. The articles include extensive photographs, children's work, and some video clips, which can be downloaded for use in training. Some of the projects discussed in past issues include The Combine Project: An Experience in a Dual-Language Classroom, spring 2001; Purposeful Learning: A Study of Water, fall 2001; and The Hairy Head Project, fall 2000.

STUDYING OTHER TEACHERS' PROJECTS

One of the best ways to learn how to do projects is to experience vicariously the project process in other classrooms. These resources provide sources of project work for study and discussion.

Beneke, Sallee. (1998). *Rearview Mirror: Reflections on a Preschool Car Project.* Available from ERIC Clearinghouse on Elementary and Early Childhood Education. University of Illinois at Urbana-Champaign, Children's Research Center, 51 Gerty Drive, Champaign, IL 61820-7469. 91pp.

This book documents the work of a preschool teacher and her coteachers, student teachers, and very young students as they explored the automotive laboratory adjacent to their early childhood classroom at a community college. Reflection about decision making in the project process makes this especially helpful for teachers learning to follow children's lead in project work.

Chard, Sylvia. (2000). *The Project Approach: Taking a Closer Look.* [CD-ROM] Can be ordered from Sylvia.Chard@ualberta.ca.

Seven projects illustrated by several hundred photographs of project work in progress and samples of children's work are presented on this CD. It also provides a structural framework for planning, implementing, and evaluating project work with specific reference to the sample projects.

Helm, Judy Harris (Ed.). (2000). *The Project Approach Catalogs.* Available from ERIC Clearinghouse on Elementary and Early Childhood Education, University of Illinois at Urbana-Champaign, Children's Research Center, 51 Gerty Drive, Champaign, IL 61820-7469. 143pp.

The three project catalogs—*Project Catalog*, 1996; *Project Catalog 2*, 1998; and *Project Catalog 3*, 2000—were written to accompany "An Evening of Sharing" events at the NAEYC's annual conferences. The catalogs provide a wealth of advice from practitioners on how to do projects, ERIC searches on research related to project work, and descriptions of each project on display at the event that year. They are a good way to learn about a variety of topics and how they might progress in classrooms for children ages toddler through third grade.

Project Catalog 1 & 2 are out of print but accessible on line in at http://ericeece.org. *Project Catalog 3* can be ordered from the ERIC Clearinghouse.

DOCUMENTATION

Documentation of project work provides information needed by the teacher for making key decisions during the project process, evidence of children's learning for child assessment, and evaluation of the project process.

Helm, Judy Harris; Beneke, Sallee; & Steinheimer, Kathy. (1998). *Windows on Learning: Documenting Young Children's Work.* Early Childhood Education Series. Available from Teachers College Press, P.O. Box 20, Williston, VT 05495-0200. 203pp.

This book presents a framework for authentic assessment and documentation in early childhood classrooms, preschool through grade three. A framework of three windows provides a structure for thinking about what to document and how to collect it, learn from it, and share it. Complete documentation for the Mail Project is shared with documentation techniques used in the project highlighted. A video also available from Teachers College Press, *Windows on Learning: A Framework for Decision-Making*, shows the documentation process at Valeska Hinton Early Childhood Education Center.

USING INTERNET RESOURCES

Internet resources, including project listservs, are discussed in Appendix A.

The Project Approach, Popular Topic web site, http://ericeece.org/project.html.

This web site provides links to many resources on project work, including Sylvia Chard's Project Approach Home Page, ERIC/EECE Digests on project work, publications such as the Project Catalogs, the Project Listserv, and journal articles on project work.

About the Editors and Contributors

Judy Harris Helm, Ed.D., has her own consulting and training company, Best Practices, Inc. Dr. Helm began her career teaching first grade and then taught, directed, and designed early childhood and primary programs and trained teachers at the community college, undergraduate, and graduate levels. She served on the Task Force for the design of Valeska Hinton Early Childhood Education Center, a state-of-the-art urban collaboration school for children age three through first grade in Peoria, Illinois, where she became Professional Development Coordinator for the school. She is former state president of the Illinois Association for the Education of Young Children. Dr. Helm is co-author of *Windows on Learning: Documenting Children's Work* and *Young Investigators: The Project Approach in the Early Years,* both published by Teachers College Press. She is also editor of *The Project Catalog I, II, and III,* published by ERIC Clearinghouse on Elementary & Early Childhood Education.

Sallee Beneke, M.Ed., has been active in early childhood education for over twenty-five years as a center director, master teacher, prekindergarten at-risk teacher, early childhood special education teacher, and head teacher in several child care centers. She is a member of the Early Childhood Education faculty at Illinois Valley Community College in Oglesby, Illinois, where she is also the Director of the Early Childhood Center featured in this publication. Ms. Beneke is author of *Rearview Mirror: Reflections on a Preschool Car Project* and co-author of *Windows on Learning: Documenting Children's Work* and *Teacher Materials for Documenting Young Children's Work.* She graduated from Cornell College, Mt. Vernon, Iowa, and completed her graduate work in Curriculum and Instruction at the University of Illinois.

Sharon Doubet, M.Ed., has been an Early Childhood Resource Specialist for Illinois StarNet Regions I and III for seven years; StarNet is operated by Western Illinois University's Center for Best Practices in Early Childhood Education under a grant from the Illinois State Board of Education. She holds a bachelor's and master's degree in Early Childhood Education. Her classroom experience includes child care and public school programs. Ms. Doubet has enjoyed a variety of positions in her 27 years in the early childhood field, including program director, teacher, grant writer, professional development facilitator, special educator, parent educator, and home visitor.

Mary Ann Gottlieb, M.S., has worked with young children throughout her teaching career. She recently left the Valeska Hinton Early Childhood Center in Peoria, Illinois, after eight years of teaching multi-age pre-kindergarten/kindergarten and kindergarten/first grade. She is currently teaching the Curiosity Corner, a Reggio-influenced toddler program at the Northminster Learning Center in Peoria. Her interests in literacy and project work have resulted in presentations at national, regional, and statewide conferences. She has also taught local literacy-related courses and continues to work as a consultant.

Amanda Helm, M.A., is a doctoral student in marketing at the University of Missouri, Columbia. She has been an instructor in marketing and communications and a newspaper reporter. Ms. Helm provides consultation and training on strategic communication, specifically the sharing of documentation with parents and other members of the community.

Lilian G. Katz, Ph.D., is Professor Emerita of Early Childhood Education at the University of Illinois at Urbana-Champaign, where she is also Co-Director of the ERIC Clearinghouse on Elementary & Early Childhood Education. Dr. Katz is author of more than one hundred articles, chapters, and books about early childhood education, teacher education, child development, and parenting. She is founding editor of the *Early Child-hood Research Quarterly* and served as Editor-in-Chief during its first six years of publication. She is currently Chair of the editorial board of the *International Journal of the Early Years,* which is published in the UK. In 1989 she wrote *Engaging Children's Minds: The Project Approach,* with S. C. Chard, which has served as a model for the project approach. Most recently she co-authored *Young Investigators: The Project Approach in the Early Years.*

Jean Lang, M.Ed., teaches three- to five-year-olds at Fairview Early Childhood Center of Rockford Public Schools. Ms. Lang has eighteen years of teaching experience in a variety of elementary and early childhood settings. She has a bachelor of science degree in Elementary Education, a master's in Learning Disabilities, and Early Childhood Endorsement with a Special Education Approval. She received a grant for introducing documentation into her school and has shared her project work at numerous conferences.

Jean O'Mara-Thieman, M.Ed., teaches a multi-age kindergarten/first grade at Valeska Hinton Early Childhood Education Center, in Peoria, Illinois. She has taught prekindergarten through sixth grade for over twenty years in a variety of settings. Ms. Thieman has a master's degree in Education from Eastern Michigan University and early childhood endorsement from Indiana University.

Dianne Rothenberg, M.S., is Director of the Illinois Early Learning Project and a cofounder of the National Parent Information Network. She is also the Co-Director of the ERIC Clearinghouse on Elementary and Early Childhood Education. Ms. Rothenberg has authored a number of journal articles, book chapters, and conference papers on topics related to her research interests: full text information online, information services for parents, information technology in education, and early childhood education. She is the former editor of two nationally marketed newsletters. Ms. Rothenberg has been involved in online educational networking since the early 1980s.

Pam Scranton, B.S., is in her seventeenth year as an early childhood educator. With a bachelor of science degree in Early Childhood Education from Bradley University, she has taught prekindergarten at both Valeska Hinton Early Childhood Education Center in Peoria, Illinois and in the Bright Beginnings program for Woodford County Special Education Association. She is currently teaching in a Reggio-inspired classroom in Northminster Learning Center's Discovery Preschool in Peoria, Illinois. Ms. Scranton's Fire Truck Project was featured in *Young Investigators: The Project Approach in the Early Years* and also in the video *A Children's Journey: The Fire Truck Project.* She provides consultation and training on the project approach and early literacy strategies.

Char Ward, Ph.D., is Grant Coordinator for Star-Net Regions I and III, an Early Childhood Technical Assistance Training Project funded by the Illinois State Board of Education and implemented through Western Illinois University (WIU). She is also a moderator and executive producer of *APPLES Magazine,* a satellite television program presented over the WIU Satellite Television Network. Dr. Ward has taught graduate and undergraduate courses at WIU, presented at national conferences on early childhood topics, and served on numerous state early childhood committees and initiatives.

Cathy Wiggers, M.S., is principal of Valeska Hinton Early Childhood Education Center. She has worked as an elementary teacher for twelve years, as an early childhood special education teacher for two years, and as an early childhood administrator for twelve years. Ms. Wiggins also serves as an Adjunct Professor at Bradley University, where she teaches courses in early childhood education and provides training and consultation to other early childhood programs for at-risk children.

Rebecca A. Wilson, B.S., is a dual-language teacher in a kindergarten classroom in West Liberty, Iowa, where she has taught for three years. She received a grant to integrate the project approach into the dual-language approach. Ms. Wilson also has experience in the child care setting and provides training and consultation to various local child care centers, Head Start, and programs on dual-language teaching in early childhood and the project approach. She is author of "The Combine Project: An Experience in a Dual Language Classroom," in the online journal *Early Childhood Research and Practice.*

Marilyn Worsley, A.A., is Lead Teacher and Assistant Director for the Illinois Valley Community College (IVCC) Early Childhood Education Center in Oglesby, Illinois. Ms. Worsley has been an early childhood educator for five years. She earned her associate's degree at IVCC, where she continues to study. She has shared her knowledge and experiences in implementing the project approach in many ways, including in *Project Approach Catalog 3.*

Maxine Wortham, Ph.D., is Executive Director of Early Childhood Programs for Peoria Public Schools in Peoria, Illinois, where she was involved in the development of Valeska Hinton Early Childhood Education Center. Dr. Wortham has worked as an elementary teacher for 10 years and as an administrator for 24 years. She is also an Adjunct Professor at Bradley University, where she teaches courses in elementary education.

Index

Numbers in **bold** indicate figures.

Accountability, 8, 79, 100
Airplane Project, 20–32
 Phase I, 25–28
 Phase II, 28–32
 Phase III, 32
Assessment, 80, 84, 88, 90–91, 97–99, 101
At-risk children, 4, 20, 39, 54, 57, 112. *See also* Poverty; Special needs, children with

Bakery Project, 35, 40
Beneke, Sallee, 97, 99
Berg, Stacy, 38
Bianchi's Pizza Parlor, 88–90, 92, **7.16**
Bike Shop Project, 14–15, **2.2**
Bilingual education, 3–5, 64–65, 67–68, 70–71
Bird Project, 54–55, 57–63
 Phase I, 58–59
 Phase II, 59–62
 Phase III, 62
Bloom, Lois, 19
Books, child-made, 35–37, 48, 53, 62, 68, 103, 106
Books, topic-related, 25, 35, 41–43, 48, 58–59, 103
Bright Beginnings, 57
Brochures, child-made, 38

Cagle, Judy, 37–38
Carle, Eric, 20
Ceiling work, 97–98, 101
Challenges, 2–5, 8, 10, 17, 79, 98–101, 104–5, 109, 112–13. *See also* Literacy; Poverty; Second-language learners; Special needs, children with; Standards
 and curriculum, 3, 5–7
 and project approach, 2–3, 7–8
Child care, 4, 11, 50–51, 99
Classroom library, 36
Cognitive skills, development of, 10, 15, 53–54, **5.3**
Combine Project, 66–69
Communication skills, 23, 40, 49, **5.2**
Community involvement, 20, 65, 78, 91, 95, 99–100, 109–11
Constructions, 23–24, 28–32, 38, 40, 46–49, 52, **5.2**, 53–55, **5.4**, **5.5**, **5.6**, 59–61, 67,

74–76, 83, 85, 88, 91–92, **7.16**, 95, 98, 106–8
Crider-Olcott, Beth, 97
Culminating activity, 11, **2.1**, 15, 21, 40–41, 45, 47–49, 62, 70, 77, 92, **7.16**, 107–8
Culture, of children, 21–22, 25, 34, 64–65, 69, 77, 79, 105
Curriculum, 1, 13, 17, **2.3**, 22–23, 42, 55, 57, 65, 79, 80–81, 83–86, 88, 90–91, 98–99, 101, 106–7, 111, 113
 and challenges, 3, 5–7, 50

Dellitt, Jaynene, 42
Demonstrations, 65–67, 71–74, 76
Developmentally Appropriate Practice (Bredekamp), 79
Developmentally Appropriate Practice in Early Childhood Programs (Bredekamp & Copple), 79
Documentation, 8, 21–22, 25, 32, 49, 60, 62, 76, 81–84, 86, 89, 97–101, 108–11
Domains of learning, 83–84, 87, 90–92
Dramatic play, 28, 32, 39–41, 66–68, 71, 74–76, 83, 85, 88–91, 107
Dual-language programs, 3, 6, 64–65, 69–71, 99

Eager to Learn (National Academy of Sciences), 13
Early childhood education
 and challenges, 2, 5
 design of, 10–11
 long-term goals of, 10, 11–17, 97
 and project approach, 7–8, 10–11
Early Learning Standards, 86
Education for All Handicapped Act, 50
ELL. *See* English-language learners
E-mail, 38, 108
Emery Air Charter, 28
Emotional development, 10, 21, 25, 32, 54–55, **5.4**, 91
English as a second language (ESL), 1, 3, 64–65, 67–68, 70–71
English-language learners (ELL), 64
Environment, of children, 21–22, 65
ESL. *See* English as a second language
Esquivel, Berta, 71

Eureka College, 58, 61
Expert visitors, 14, **2.1**, 28, 41, 44, **5.2**, 59, 61, 66–67, 108, 112

Fairview Early Childhood Center, 25
Farm Project, 35–36, 38–40, 51
Field–site visits, 11, 21–24, 28–30, 36, 41, 44, **5.3**, 54, **5.4**, 55, 66–67, 69–74, 78, 82–83, 89–91, **7.16**, 106–8, 111–12
Fine motor skills, 55, **5.5**, 58, 60–61
Fire Station Project, 67–69, 113
Flori, Veronica, 86, 88–91
FLYKIDS, 32
Formal instruction, 13–14, 22–23
Frieman, Deb, 25, 27

Garden Project, 68–69
Granados, Lupe, 86
Griffin, Ellen, 57
Grocery Store Project, 1, 40
Gross motor skills, 55–56, **5.6**, 59–60

Head Start, 8, 57
Health Center Project, 36–37, 41
Helm, Judy, 7, 10, 81, 98, 105, 113
Hi, Pizza Man! (Walter), 89, **7.16**
Hyperstudio, 107

IDEA. *See* Individuals with Disabilities Education Act
IEP. *See* Individual Education Plan
Illinois Early Learning Standards, 25, 57, 80–81, 83, 86, 89, 91, 95
Illinois Project Group, 86
Illinois River, 42–44
Illinois School Report Card, 57
Illinois Valley Center, 81
Individual Education Plan (IEP), 1, 50–58, **5.2**, **5.3**, **5.4**, **5.5**, **5.6**, 60–61
Individualized teaching, 84, 87, 90
Individuals with Disabilities Education Act (IDEA), 3, 50–51
Intellectual dispositions, 16, 20–22, 24, 26, 29, 32, 53, 58, 98, 104
IVCC Early Childhood Education Center, 86

Johnson, Kendrya', 42

Katz, Lilian, 6, 7, 81, 98, 105, 113
Kidspiration, 107
Kids Pix Studio Deluxe, 107
Kindergarten, 4, 7, 11, 13, 22, 58, 77, 80

La Mexicana Restaurant, 71–78
Language development, 52–53, **5.2**. *See also* Literacy; Vocabulary, development of
Language-rich play, 39–40, 46–48, 68
Leadership skills, development of, 23, 47
Learning centers, 7, 44, 50–51, 106–7
Library Project, 85
Light Project, 40
Linguistic skills, development of, 15, 36, 44
Listening skills, development of, 41, 44–45, 52, 54, 107
Literacy, 2–3, 7, 16, 23–24, 26, 28, 34, 52, 60, 65, 79, 89, 98, 100, 106, 109. *See also* Project approach, and literacy; Water to River Project
    and socioeconomic status, 11, 13–14, 19–20

Mail Project, 36
Mathematical skills, 20, 77, 91, **7.16**, 98
McCulloh, Bob, 25, 27
Meadow Project, 84
Mentoring, 23, 26–27, 37, 40, 45, 47–49, 51, 56, 86
Mexican Restaurant Project, 24, 66, 68–78
    Phase I, 71
    Phase II, 71–76
    Phase III, 76–77
Modeling, 65, 67–68, 71, 74, 76, 78
Motivation, during project work, 84–85, 89–91
Musical Instruments Project, 83

NAEYC. *See* National Association for the Education of Young Children
National Assessment Governing Board, 2–3
National Association for the Education of Young Children (NAEYC), 1–3, 36, 80
National Council of Teachers of Mathematics, 80
National Education Goals Panel, 80
Native language, 65, 69, 74, 77

Open house, 38, 53

Parental involvement, 7, 20–21, 23, 25, 28–30, 33–35, 37, 42, 50, 57–58, 65, 69–70, 77, 86, 92, 98–101, 105–6, 108–9, 111–12
Paydarfar, David, 103–4
Pedagogy, 99
Peer coaching. *See* Mentoring
Phase I, 11, **2.1**, 15, 23, 52, 83, 106, 108
Phase II, 11, **2.1**, 14–15, 52, 106, 108, 110
Phase III, 11, **2.1**, 14–15, 40, 53, 108, 110
Phonics, 16, 35
Photographs, of field-site visits, 30, 35–36, 39, 44, **5.4**, 59, 61, 74, 76, 82, 89, 91, 98, 107–8
Pizza Project, 81, **7.1**, **7.2**, **7.3**, 89–95
    Phase I, 87–89
    Phase II, 89–92
    Phase III, 92
Planning web, 25–26, **3.2**, **3.4**, 35, 43, **4.7**, 52, 68–69, 71, 81, **7.1**, **7.2**, 82–83, **7.3**, **7.4**, **7.7**, 87, 89, 95, 97–98, 101, 106–9

Playground Project, 55
Potato Project, 55
Poverty, 2, 4–5, 7, 79, 100. *See also* Airplane Project; Project approach, and poverty effects of, 19–20
Preschool, 4, 7, 11, 13–14, 50–51, 79, 109
Problem-solving skills, 23, 25–26, 32, 53–55, **5.4**, 58–59, 61, 75, 83–84, 91–92, **7.16**, 98, 100, 107
Project approach. *See also* Community involvement; Constructions; Culminating activity; Documentation; Expert visitors; Field-site visits; Parental involvement; Phase I; Phase II; Phase III; Planning Web; Questions; Sketching; Word wall
    and challenges, 2–3, 7–8. *See also* Literacy; Poverty; Second-language learners; Special needs, children with; Standards
    and children with special needs, 50–63
        practical strategies, 51–57. *See also individual strategies*
    and curriculum, 1, 3, 7, 17
    definition of project, 11, 113
    in early childhood education, 7–8, 10–11
    for laying good education foundations, 10–17
    and literacy, 14, 35–49
        practical strategies, 35–42. *See also individual strategies*
    planning for, 97–98
    and poverty, 19–33
        practical strategies, 20–25. *See also individual strategies*
    and school administrators, 57, 86, 98, 101, 108, 111–12
    and second-language learners, 64–78
        practical strategies, 65–71. *See also individual strategies*
    selection of topic, 11, **2.1**, 14–15, 17, 20–22, 25, 42, 58, 71, 78, 83, 87, 92, **7.16**, 106
    and standards, 79–95
        practical strategies, 80–86. *See also individual strategies*
    training for, 111–13

Questions, 21–22, 26, **3.4**, 28, 35, 37–38, 40–42, 44, 49, 52, **5.4**, 58–59, 61, 65, 67–69, 71–74, 76, 88, **7.16**, 103–4

Rearview Mirror (Beneke), 99, 113
Reference materials, 24, 37–39, 44, 46, 48–49, 58–59, 68, 106, 109
Reflective dispositions, 15
Reggio Emilia, 7, 97, 99
Resiliency, 5–6, 20–21, 23–24, 98, 100
Riollano, Kaleena, 86
Role-play, 65, 67–68, 71, 74, 76, 78

Salazar, Teresa, 71
Schwartz, William J., 103–4
Scranton, Pam, 38
Second-language learners, 2–4, 7, 21, 34, 64–65, 79, 100, 105, 109. *See also* Bilingual education; Dual-language programs; English as a second language; Mexican Restaurant Project; Project approach, and second-language learners

Self-confidence, 20, 77, 98
Self-efficacy, 5
Self-esteem, 5, 20, 24
Self-image, 20, 33
Self-initiated learning, 20–21, 25, 29, 33, 98
Sheep Project, 21–23
Sketching, 26, 28, 39–40, 44, 55, **5.5**, 60, 63, 71–74, 83, 85, 87–88, 90, **7.16**, 95, 98, 104, 108, 110
Small-group discussion, 52–53, 58–59
Social skills, development of, 10, 15, 17, 22–23, 25–26, 32, 54–55, **5.4**, 91
Socioeconomic status, 11, 13–14, 19–20, 32. *See also* Literacy, and socioeconomic status; Poverty
Special needs, children with, 1–5, 7, 25, 50–51, 79, 100, 105, 108–9, 112. *See also* Bird Project; Project approach, and children with special needs
Speech, development of, 52–53, **5.2**
Standards, 1–3, 7, 25, **3.2**, 49, 79–83, 89, 97, 100–101, 106–7, 112. *See also* Pizza Project; Project approach, and standards
Star Teachers of Children in Poverty (Haberman), 4
Storm, The (Cowley), 43

Teaching on the fly, 98
Technology, 107–8
Television, 4

Umbrella (Cowley), 43
U.S. Census Bureau, 19

Valeska Hinton Early Childhood Education Center, 35, 42, 97
Vet Project, 54
Videos, of field-site visits, 28–29, 36, 39, 67, 91, 107–8
Vocabulary development of, 23, 35–36, 39, 41–44, 47, 52–53, **5.2**, **5.4**, 58, 60, 62, 68–69, 103, 106
Vollmer, Mary Ann, 86

Water to River Project, 42–49, 106–7
    Phase I, 42–44
    Phase II, 44–48
    Phase III, 48–49
West Liberty Elementary School, 65, 71
What's It Like to Be a Fish? (Pfeffer, Keller, & Keller), 43
Who Eats What (Lauber & Keller), 43
Wilson, Rebecca, 6, 97
Windows on Learning (Helm), 101, 113
Word wall, 39, 48, 52, **5.2**, 55, 60–62, 68
Work Sampling Assessment System, 25, 49, 54, 57, 60, 80, 84, 86, 99, 106
Worsley, Marilyn, 81
Writing skills, development of, 24, 37–40, 43–45, 48–49, 52–53, 55, **5.5**, 59–63, 65, 71, 73–75, 77, 80, 85, 88, 91, 98, 107

Young Investigators (Helm and Katz), 7, 81, 98, 105, 113

Zecca, Kathie, 86
Zoo Project, 39–40